NEGRO FOLK RHYMES

Wise and Otherwise

WITH A STUDY

BY

THOMAS W. TALLEY

OF FISK UNIVERSITY

ISBN: 978-1-63923-752-4

Printed: February 2023

Published and Distributed By:
Lushena Books
607 Country Club Drive, Unit E
Bensenville, IL 60106
www.lushenabks.com

ISBN: 978-1-63923-752-4

INTRODUCTION

Of the making of books by individual authors there is no end; but a cultivated literary taste among the exceptional few has rendered almost impossible the production of genuine folk-songs. The spectacle, therefore, of a homogeneous throng of partly civilized people dancing to the music of crude instruments and evolving out of dance-rhythm a lyrical or narrative utterance in poetic form is sufficiently rare in the nineteenth century to challenge immediate attention. In *Negro Folk Rhymes* is to be found no inconsiderable part of the musical and poetic life-records of a people; the compiler presents an arresting volume which, in addition to being a pioneer and practically unique in its field, is as nearly exhaustive as a sympathetic understanding of the Negro mind, careful research, and labor of love can make it. Professor Talley of Fisk University has spared himself no pains in collecting and piecing together every attainable scrap and fragment of secular rhyme which might help in adequately interpreting the inner life of his own people.

INTRODUCTION

Being the expression of a race in, or just emerging from bondage, these songs may at first seem to some readers trivial and almost wholly devoid of literary merit. In phraseology they may appear crude, lacking in that elegance and finish ordinarily associated with poetic excellence; in imagery they are at times exceedingly winter-starved, mediocre, common, drab, scarcely ever rising above the unhappy environment of the singers. The outlook upon life and nature is, for the most part, one of imaginative simplicity and child-like naïveté; superstitions crowd in upon a worldly wisdom that is elementary, practical, and obvious; and a warped and crooked human nature, developed and fostered by circumstances, shows frequently through the lines. What else might be expected? At the time when these rhymes were in process of being created the conditions under which the American Negro lived and labored were not calculated to inspire him with a desire for the highest artistic expression. Restricted, cramped, bound in unwilling servitude, he looked about him in his miserable little world to see whatever of the beautiful or happy he might find; that which he discovered is pathetically slight, but, such as it is, it served to keep alive his stunted artist-soul under the most adverse circumstances.

He saw the sweet pinks under a blue sky, or observed the fading violets and the roses that fall, as he passed to a tryst under the oak trees of a forest, and wrought these things into his songs of love and tenderness. Friendless and otherwise without companionship he lived in imagination with the beasts and birds of the great out-of-doors; he knew personally Mr. Coon, Brother Rabbit, Mr. 'Possum and their associates of the wild; Judge Buzzard and Sister Turkey appealed to his fancy as offering material for what he supposed to be poetic treatment. Wherever he might find anything in his lowly position which seemed to him truly useful or beautiful, he seized upon it and wove about it the sweetest song he could sing. The result is not so much poetry of a high order as a valuable illustration of the persistence of artist-impulses even in slavery.

In some of these folk-songs, however, may be found certain qualities which give them dignity and worth. They are, when properly presented, rhythmical to the point of perfection. I myself have heard many of them chanted with and without the accompaniment of clapping hands, stamping feet, and swaying bodies. Unfortunately a large part of their liquid melody and flexibility of movement is lost through confinement in cold print; but when they are heard from a distance on quiet summer nights or clear Southern mornings, even the most fastidious ear is satisfied with the rhythmic pulse of them. That pathos of the Negro character which can never be quite adequately caught in words or transcribed in music is then augmented and intensified by the peculiar quality of the Negro voice, rich in overtones, quavering, weird, cadenced, throbbing with the sufferings of a race. Or perhaps that well-developed sense of humor which has, for more than a century, made ancestral sorrows bearable finds fuller expression in the lilting turn of a note than in the flashes of wit which abundantly enliven the pages of this volume. There is one lyric in particular which, in evident sincerity of feeling, simple and unaffected grace, and regularity of form, appeals to me as having intrinsic literary value:

She hug' me, an' she kiss' me,
She wrung my han' an' cried.
She said I wus de sweetes' thing
Dat ever lived or died.

She hug' me an' she kiss' me.
Oh Heaben! De touch o' her han'!
She said I wus de puttiest thing
In de shape o' mortal man.

I told her dat I love' her,
Dat my love wus bed-cord strong;
Den I axed her w'en she'd have me,
An' she jes' say, "Go 'long!"

There is also a dramatic quality about many of these rhymes which must not be overlooked. It has long been my observation that the Negro is possessed by nature of considerable, though not as yet highly developed, histrionic ability; he takes delight in acting out in pantomime whatever he may be relating in song or story. It is not surprising, then, to find that the play-rhymes, originating from the "call" and "response," are really little dramas when presented in their proper settings. "Caught By The Witch" would not be ineffective if, on a dark night, it were acted in the vicinity of a graveyard! And one ballad—if I may be permitted to dignify it by that name—called "Promises of Freedom" is characterized by an unadorned narrative style and a dramatic ending which are associated with the best English folk-ballads. The singer tells simply and, one feels, with a grim impersonality of how his mistress promised to set him free; it seemed as if she would never die—but "she's somehow gone"! His master likewise made promises,

Yes, my ole Mosser promise' me;
But "his papers" didn't leave me free.
A dose of pizen he'pped 'im along.
May de Devil preach 'is funer'l song.

The manner of this conclusion is strikingly like that of the Scottish ballad, "Edward,"

The curse of hell frae me sall ye beir,
Mither, Mither,
The curse of hell frae me sall ye beir,
Sic counseils ye gave to me O.

In both a story of cruelty is suggested in a single artistic line and ended with startling, dramatic abruptness.

In fact, these two songs probably had their ultimate origin in not widely dissimilar types of illiterate, unsophisticated human society. Professor Talley's "Study in Negro Folk Rhymes," appended to this volume of songs, is illuminating. One may not be disposed to accept without considerable modification his theories entire; still his account from personal, first-hand knowledge of the beginnings and possible evolution of certain rhymes in this collection is apparently authentic. Here we have again, in the nineteenth century, the record of a singing, dancing people creating by a process approximating communal authorship a mass of verse embodying tribal memories, ancestral superstitions, and racial wisdom handed down from generation to generation through oral tradition. These are genuine folk-songs—lyrics, ballads, rhymes—in which are crystallized the thought and feeling, the universally shared lore of a folk. Recent theorizers on poetic origins who would insist upon individual as opposed to community authorship of certain types of song-narrative might do well to consider Professor Talley's characteristic study. And students of comparative literature who love to recreate the life of a tribe or nation from its song and story will discover in this collection a mine of interesting material.

Fisk University, the center of Negro culture in America, is to be congratulated upon having initiated the gathering and preservation of these relics, a valuable heritage from the past. Just how important for literature this heritage may prove to be will not appear until this institution—and others with like purposes—has fully developed by cultivation, training, and careful fostering the artistic impulses so abundantly a part of the Negro character. A race which has produced, under the most disheartening conditions, a mass of folk-poetry such as *Negro Folk Rhymes* may be expected to create, with unlimited opportunities for self-development, a literature and a distinctive music of superior quality.

WALTER CLYDE CURRY.

Vanderbilt University,
September 30, 1921.

PART I

NEGRO FOLK RHYMES

Dance Rhyme Section

JONAH'S BAND PARTY

Setch a kickin' up san'! Jonah's Ban'!
Setch a kickin' up san'! Jonah's Ban'!
"Han's up sixteen! Circle to de right!
We's gwine to git big eatin's here to-night."

Setch a kickin' up san'! Jonah's Ban'!
Setch a kickin' up san'! Jonah's Ban'!
"Raise yo' right foot, kick it up high,
Knock dat * Mobile Buck in de eye."

Setch a kickin' up san'! Jonah's Ban'!
Setch a kickin' up san'! Jonah's Ban'!
"Stan' up, flat foot, * Jump dem Bars!
* Karo back'ards lak a train o' kyars."

Setch a kickin' up san'! Jonah's Ban'!
Setch a kickin' up san'! Jonah's Ban'!
"Dance 'round, Mistiss, show 'em de p'int;
Dat Nigger don't know how to * Coonjaint."

* These are dance steps. For explanation read the Study in Negro Folk Rhymes.

LOVE IS JUST A THING OF FANCY

LOVE is jes a thing o' fancy,
Beauty's jes a blossom;
If you wants to git yō' finger bit,
Stick it at a 'possum.

Beauty, it's jes skin deep;
Ugly, it's to de bone.
Beauty, it'll jes fade 'way;
But Ugly'll hōl' 'er own.

STILL WATER CREEK

'WAY down yon'er on Still Water Creek,
I got stalded an' stayed a week.
I see'd Injun Puddin and Punkin pie,
But de black cat stick 'em in de yaller cat's eye.

'Way down yon'er on Still Water Creek,
De Niggers grows up some ten or twelve feet.
Dey goes to bed but dere hain't no use,
Caze deir feet sticks out fer de chickens t' roost.

I got hongry on Still Water Creek,
De mud to de hub an' de hoss britchin weak.
I stewed bullfrog chitlins, baked polecat pie;
If I goes back dar, I shō's gwine to die.

NEGRO FOLK RHYMES

'POSSUM UP THE GUM STUMP

'Possum up de gum stump,
Dat raccoon in de holler;
Twis' 'im out, an' git 'im down,
An' I'll gin you a half a doller.

'Possum up de gum stump,
Yes, cooney in de holler;
A pretty gal down my house
Jes as fat as she can waller.

'Possum up de gum stump,
His jaws is black an' dirty;
To come an' kiss you, pretty gal,
I'd run lak a gobbler tucky.

'Possum up de gum stump,
A good man's hard to fīn';
You'd better love me, pretty gal,
You'll git de yudder kīn'.

JOE AND MALINDA JANE

OLE Joe jes swore upon 'is life
He'd make Merlindy Jane 'is wife.
W'en she hear 'im up 'is love an' tell,
She jumped in a bar'l o' mussel shell.
She scrape 'er back till de skin come off.
Nex' day she die wid de Whoopin' Cough.

WALK, TALK, CHICKEN WITH YOUR HEAD PECKED!

WALK, talk, chicken wid yō' head pecked!
You can crow w'en youse been dead.
Walk, talk, chicken wid yō' head pecked!
You can hōl' high yō' bloody head.

You's whooped dat Blue Hen's Chicken,
You's beat 'im at his game.
If dere's some fedders on him,
Fer dat you's not to blame.

Walk, talk, chicken wid yō' head pecked!
You beat ole Johnny Blue!
Walk, talk, chicken wid yō' head pecked!
Say: "Cock-a-doo-dle-doo—!"

TAILS

De coon's got a long ringed bushy tail,
De 'possum's tail is bare;
Dat rabbit hain't got no tail 'tall,
'Cep' a liddle bunch o' hair.

De gobbler's got a big fan tail,
De pattridge's tail is small;
Dat peacock's tail 's got great big
eyes,
But dey don't see nothin' 'tall.

CAPTAIN DIME

Cappun Dime is a fine w'ite man.
He wash his face in a fry'n' pan,
He comb his head wid a waggin wheel,
An' he die wid de toothache in his heel.

Cappun Dime is a mighty fine feller,
An' he shō' play kyards wid de Niggers in
de cellar,
But he will git drunk, an' he **won't** smoke a
pipe,
Den he will pull de watermillions 'fore dey
gits ripe.

CROSSING THE RIVER

I WENT down to de river an' I couldn' git 'cross.
I jumped on er mule an' I thought 'e wus er hoss.
Dat mule 'e wa'k in an' git mired up in de san';
You'd oughter see'd dis Nigger make back fer de
lan'!

I want to cross de river but I caint git 'cross;
So I mounted on a ram, fer I thought 'e wus er hoss.
I plunged him in, but he sorter fail to swim;
An' I give five dollars fer to git 'im out ag'in.

Yes, I went down to de river an' I couldn' git 'cross,
So I give a whole dollar fer a ole blin' hoss;
Den I souzed him in an' he sink 'stead o' swim.
Do you know I got wet clean to my ole hat brim?

T-U-TURKEY

T-u, tucky, T-u, ti.
T-u, tucky, buzzard's eye.
T-u, tucky, T-u, ting.
T-u, tucky, buzzard's wing.
Oh, Mistah Washin'ton! Don't whoop me,
Whoop dat Nigger Back 'hind dat tree.

He stole tucky, I didn' steal none.
Go wuk him in de co'n field jes fer fun.

CHICKEN IN THE BREAD TRAY

"AUNTIE, will yō' dog bite?"—
"No, Chile! No!"
Chicken in de bread tray
A makin' up dough.

"Auntie, will yō' broom hit?"—
"Yes, Chile!" Pop!
Chicken in de bread tray;
"Flop! Flop! Flop!"

"Auntie, will yō' oven bake?"—
"Yes. Jes fry!"—
"What's dat chicken good fer?"—
"Pie! Pie! Pie!"

"Auntie, is yō' pie good?"—
"Good as you could 'spec'."
Chicken in de bread tray;
"Peck! Peck! Peck!"

MOLLY COTTONTAIL, OR, GRAVEYARD RABBIT

OLE Molly Cottontail,
At night, w'en de moon's pale;
You don't fail to tu'n tail,
You always gives me leg bail.*

Molly in de Bramble-brier,
Let me git a little nigher;
Prickly-pear, it sting lak fire!
Do please come pick out de brier!

Molly in de pale moonlight,
Yō' tail is shō a pretty white;
You takes it fer 'way out'n sight.
"Molly! Molly! Molly Bright!"

Ole Molly Cottontail,
You sets up on a rotten rail!
You tears through de graveyard!
You makes dem ugly † hants wail.

Ole Molly Cottontail,
Won't you be shore not to fail

* Leg bail = to run away.
† Hants = ghosts or spirits.

* To give me yō' right hīn' foot?
My luck, it won't be fer sale.

†JUBA

JUBA dis, an' Juba dat,
Juba ‡skin dat Yaller Cat. Juba! Juba!

Juba jump an' Juba sing.
Juba, ‡cut dat Pigeon's Wing. Juba! Juba!

Juba, kick off Juba's shoe.
Juba, dance dat ‡Jubal Jew. Juba! Juba!

Juba, whirl dat foot about.
Juba, blow dat candle out. Juba! Juba!

Juba circle, ‡Raise de Latch.
Juba do dat ‡Long Dog Scratch. Juba! Juba!

* This embraces the old superstition that carrying in one's pocket the right hind foot of a rabbit, which has habitually lived about a cemetery, brings good luck to its possessor.

† This peculiar kind of dance rhyme is explained in the Study in Negro Folk Rhymes.

‡ The expressions marked ‡ are various kinds of dance steps.

ON TOP OF THE POT

WILD goose gallop an' gander trot;
Walk about, Mistiss, on top o' de pot!

Hog jowl bilin', an' tunnup greens hot,
Walk about, Billie, on top o' de pot!

Chitlins, hog years, all on de spot,
Walk about, ladies, on top o' de pot!

* STAND BACK, BLACK MAN

Oh!

STAN' back, black man,
You cain't shine;
Yō' lips is too thick,
An' you hain't my kīn'.

* In a few places in the South, just following the Civil War, the Mulattoes organized themselves into a little guild known as "The Blue Vein Circle," from which those who were black were excluded. This is one of their rhymes.

Aw!

Git 'way, black man,
You jes haint fine;
I'se done quit foolin'
Wid de nappy-headed kind.

Say?

Stan' back, black man!
Cain't you see
Dat a kinky-headed chap
Hain't nothin' side o' me?

NEGROES NEVER DIE

NIGGER! Nigger never die!
He gits choked on Chicken pie.
Black face, white shiny eye. Nigger! Nigger!

Nigger! Nigger never knows!
Mashed nose, an' crooked toes;
Dat's de way de Nigger goes. Nigger! Nigger!

Nigger! Nigger always sing;
Jump up, cut de Pidgeon's wing;
Whirl, an' give his feet a fling. Nigger! Nigger!

JAWBONE

SAMSON, shout! Samson, moan!
Samson, bring on yō' Jawbone.

Jawbone, walk! Jawbone, talk!
Jawbone, eat wid a knife an fo'k.

Walk, Jawbone! Jinny, come alon'!
Yon'er goes Sally wid de bootees on.

Jawbone, ring! Jawbone, sing!
Jawbone, kill dat wicked thing.

INDIAN FLEA

INJUN flea, bit my knee;
Kaze I wouldn' drink ginger tea.

Flea bite hard, flea bite quick;
Flea bite burn lak dat seed tick.

Hit dat flea, flea not dere.
I'se so mad I pulls my hair.

I go wild an' fall in de creek.
To wash 'im off, I'd stay a week.

AS I WENT TO SHILOH

As I went down
To Shiloh Town;
I rolled my barrel of Sogrum down.
Dem lasses rolled;
An' de hoops, dey bust;
An' blowed dis Nigger clear to
Thundergust!

JUMP JIM CROW

Git fus upon yō' heel,
An' den upon yō' toe;
An ebry time you tu'n 'round,
You jump Jim Crow.

Now fall upon yō' knees,
Jump up an' bow low;
An' ebry time you tu'n 'round,
You jump Jim Crow.

Put yō' han's upon yō' hips,
Bow low to yō' beau;
An' ehry time you tu'n 'round,
You jump Jim Crow.

DANCE RHYME SONG SECTION

(*Use all the stanzas of "Jaybird"*)

JAYBIRD

De Jaybird jump from lim' to lim',
An' he tell Br'er Rabbit to do lak him.

Br'er Rabbit say to de cunnin' elf:
"You jes want me to fall an' kill myself."

Dat Jaybird a-settin' on a swingin' lim'.
He wink at me an' I wink at him.
He laugh at me w'en my gun "crack."
It kick me down on de flat o' my back.

Nex' day de Jaybird dance dat lim'.
I grabs my gun fer to shoot at him.
W'en I "crack" down, it split my chin.
"Ole Aggie Cunjer" fly lak sin.

Way down yon'er at de risin' sun,
Jaybird a-talkin' wid a forked tongue.
*He's been down dar whar de bad mens dwell.
"Ole Friday Devil," fare—you—well!

OFF FROM RICHMOND

I'SE off from Richmon' sooner in de mornin'.
I'se off from Richmon' befō' de break o' day.
I slips off from Mosser widout pass an' warnin'
Fer I mus' see my Donie wharever she may stay.

* A superstition. For explanation, see Study in Negro Folk Rhymes.

HE IS MY HORSE

ONE day as I wus a-ridin' by,
Said dey: "Ole man, yō' hoss will die"—
"If he dies, he is my loss;
An' if he lives, he is my hoss."

Nex' day w'en I come a-ridin' by,
Dey said: "Ole man, yō' hoss may die."—
"If he dies, I'll tan 'is skin;
An' if he lives, I'll ride 'im ag'in."

Den ag'in w'en I come a-ridin' by,
Said dey: "Ole man, yō' hoss mought
die."—
"If he dies, I'll eat his co'n;
An' if he lives, I'll ride 'im on."

* JUDGE BUZZARD

DERE sets Jedge Buzzard on de Bench.
Go tu'n him off wid a monkey wrench!
Jedge Buzzard try Br'er Rabbit's case;
An' he say Br'er Tarepin win dat race.
Here sets Jedge Buzzard on de Bench.
Knock him off wid dat monkey wrench!

* See Study in Negro Rhymes for explanation.

SHEEP AND GOAT

SHEEP an' goat gwine to de paster;
Says de goat to de sheep: "Cain't you walk a liddle faster?"

De sheep says: "I cain't, I'se a liddle too full."
Den de goat say: "You can wid my ho'ns in yō' wool."

But de goat fall down an' skin 'is shin
An' de sheep split 'is lip wid a big broad grin.

JACKSON, PUT THAT KETTLE ON!

JACKSON, put dat kittle on!
Fire, steam dat coffee done!
Day done broke, an' I got to run
Fer to meet my gal by de risin' sun.

My ole Mosser say to me,
Dat I mus' drink * sassfac tea;
But Jackson stews dat coffee done,
An' he shō' gits his po'tion: Son!

* Sassfac = sassafras.

DINAH'S DINNER HORN

It's a cōl', frosty mornin',
An' de Niggers goes to wo'k;
Wid deir axes on deir shoulders,
An' widout a bit o' * shu't.

Dey's got ole husky ashcake,
Widout a bit o' fat;
An' de white folks'll grumble,
If you eats much o' dat.

I runs down to de henhouse,
An' I falls upon my knees;
It's 'nough to make a rabbit laugh
To hear my tucky sneeze.

I grows up on dem meatskins,
I comes down on a bone;
I hits dat co'n bread fifty licks,
I makes dat butter moan.

It's glory in yō' honor!
An' don't you want to go?
I sholy will be ready
Fer dat dinnah ho'n to blow.

* Shu't = shirt.

Dat ole bell, it goes "Bangity—
bang!"
Fer all dem white folks bo'n.
But I'se not ready fer to go
Till Dinah blows her ho'n.

"Poke—sallid!" "Poke—sallid!"
Dat ole ho'n up an' blow.
Jes think about dem good ole greens!
Say? Don't you want to go?

MY MULE

Las' Saddy mornin' Mosser said:
"Jump up now, Sambo, out'n bed.
Go saddle dat mule, an' go to town;
An' bring home Mistiss' mornin'
gown."

I saddled dat mule to go to town.
I mounted up an' he buck'd me down.
Den I jumped up from out'n de dust,
An' I rid him till I thought he'd bust.

BULLFROG PUT ON THE SOLDIER CLOTHES

BULLFROG put on de soldier clo's.
He went down yonder fer to shoot at de crows;
Wid a knife an' a fo'k between 'is toes,
An' a white hankcher fer to wipe 'is nose.

Bullfrog put on de soldier clo's.
He's a "dead shore shot," gwineter kill dem crows."
He takes "Pot," an' "Skillet" from de Fiddler's Ball.
Dey're to dance a liddle jig while Jim Crow fall.

Bullfrog put on de soldier clo's.
He went down de river fer to shoot at de crows.
De powder flash, an' de crows fly 'way;
An' de Bullfrog shoot at 'em all nex' day.

SAIL AWAY, LADIES!

SAIL away, ladies! Sail away!
Sail away, ladies! Sail away!
Nev' min' what dem white folks say,
May de Mighty bless you. Sail away!

Nev' min' what yō' daddy say,
Shake yō' liddle foot an' fly away.
Nev' min' if yō' mammy say:
"De Devil'll git you." Sail away!

THE BANJO PICKING

HUSH boys! Hush boys! Don't make a noise,
While ole Mosser's sleepin'.
We'll run down de Graveyard, an' take out
de bones,
An' have a liddle Banjer pickin'.

I takes my Banjer on a Sunday mornin'.
Dem ladies, dey 'vites me to come.
We slips down de hill an' picks de liddle chune:
"Walk, Tom Wilson Here Afternoon."

*"Walk Tom Wilson Here Afternoon";
"You Cain't Dance Lak ole Zipp Coon."
Pick *"Dinah's Dinner Ho'n" "Dance 'Round
de Room."
"Sweep dat Kittle Wid a Bran' New Broom."

* Those starred are found elsewhere in this volume. We were unable to obtain the other three.

OLD MOLLY HARE

OLE Molly har'!
What's you doin' thar?
"I'se settin' in de fence corner, smokin' seegyar."

Ole Molly har'!
What's you doin' thar?
"I'se pickin' out a br'or, settin' on a Pricky-p'ar."

Ole Molly har'!
What's you doin' thar?
"I'se gwine cross de Cotton Patch, hard as I can t'ar."

Molly har' to-day,
So dey all say,
Got her pipe o' clay, jes to smoke de time 'way.

"De dogs say 'boo!'
An' dey barks too.
I hain't got no time fer to talk to you."

ONE NEGRO TUNE USED WITH "AN OPOSSUM HUNT"

AN OPOSSUM HUNT

'POSSUM meat is good an' sweet,
I always finds it good to eat.
My dog tree, I went to see.
A great big 'possum up dat tree.
I retch up an' pull him in,
Den dat ole 'possum 'gin to grin.

I tuck him home an' dressed him
off,
Dat night I laid him in de fros'.
De way I cooked dat 'possum
sound,
I fust parboiled, den baked him
brown.
I put sweet taters in de pan,
'Twus de bigges' eatin' in de lan'.

DEVILISH PIGS

I WISH I had a load o' poles,
To fence my new-groun' lot;
To keep dem liddle bitsy debblish pigs
Frum a-rootin' up all I'se got.

Dey roots my cabbage, roots my co'n;
Dey roots up all my beans.
Dey speilt my fine sweet-tater patch,
An' dey ruint my tunnup greens.

I'se rund dem pigs, an' I'se rund dem
pigs.
I'se gittin' mighty hot;
An' one dese days w'en nobody look,
Dey'll root 'round in my pot.

PROMISES OF FREEDOM

My ole Mistiss promise me,
W'en she died, she'd set me free.
She lived so long dat 'er head got bal',
An' she give out'n de notion a dyin'
at all.

My ole Mistiss say to me:
"Sambo, I'se gwine ter set you free."
But w'en dat head git slick an' bal',
De Lawd couldn' a' killed 'er wid
a big green maul.

My ole Mistiss never die,
Wid 'er nose all hooked an' skin all
dry.
But my ole Miss, she's somehow gone,
An' she lef' "Uncle Sambo" a-hillin'
up co'n.

Ole Mosser lakwise promise me,
W'en he died, he'd set me free.
But ole Mosser go an' make his Will
Fer to leave me a-plowin' ole Beck
still.

Yes, my ole Mosser promise me;
But "his papers" didn' leave me free.
A dose of pizen he'ped 'im along.
May de Devil preach 'is fūner'l song.

WHEN MY WIFE DIES

W'EN my wife dies, gwineter git me anudder one;
A big fat yaller one, jes lak de yudder one.
I'll hate mighty bad, w'en she's been gone.
Hain't no better 'oman never nowhars been bo'n.

W'en I comes to die, you mus'n' bury me deep,
But put Sogrum molasses close by my feet.
Put a pone o' co'n bread way down in my han'.
Gwineter sop on de way to de Promus' Lan'.

W'en I goes to die, Nobody mus'n' cry,
Mus'n' dress up in black, fer I mought come back.
But w'en I'se been dead, an' almos' fergotten;
You mought think about me an' keep on a-trottin'.

Railly, w'en I'se been dead, you needn' bury me at tall.
You mought pickle my bones down in alkihall;
Den fold my han's "so," right across my breas';
An' go an' tell de folks I'se done gone to "res'."

ONE TUNE USED WITH "BAA! BAA! BLACK SHEEP!"

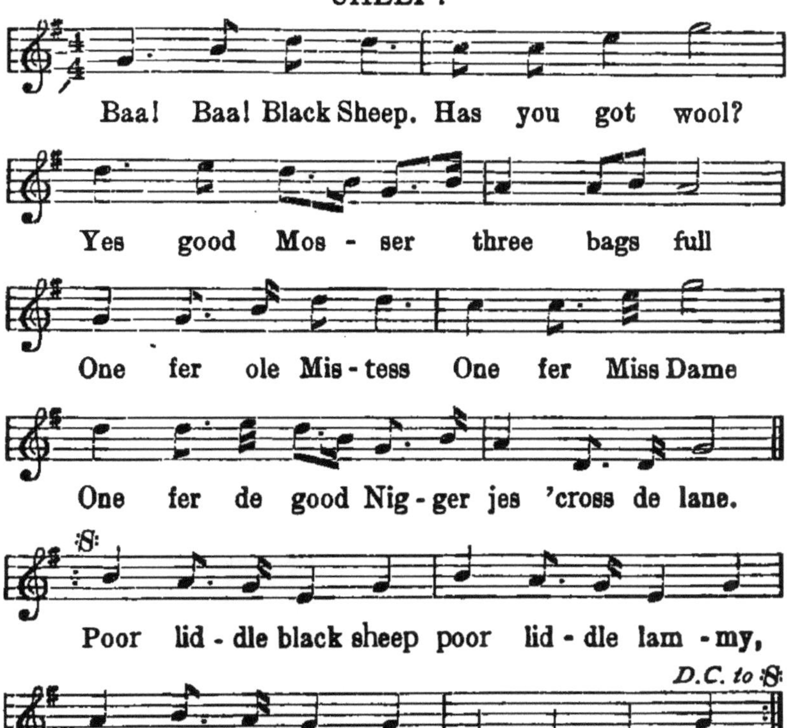

BAA! BAA! BLACK SHEEP

"Baa! Baa! Black Sheep,
Has you got wool?"
"Yes, good Mosser,
Free bags full.
One fer ole Mistis,
One fer Miss Dame,

An' one fer de good Nigger
Jes across de lane."
Pōōr liddle Black Sheep,
Pōōr liddle lammy;
Pōōr liddle Black Sheep's
Got no mammy.

HE WILL GET MR. COON

Ole Mistah Coon, at de break o' day,
You needn' think youse gwineter git 'way.
Caze ole man Ned, he know how to run,
An' he's shō' gone fer to git 'is gun.

You needn' clam to dat highes' lim',
You cain't git out'n de retch o' him.
You can stay up dar till de sun done set.
I'll bet you a dollar dat he'll git you yet.

Ole Mistah Coon, you'd well's to give up.
You had well's to give up, I say.
Caze ole man Ned is straight atter you,
An' he'll git you shō' this day.

BRING ON YOUR HOT CORN

BRING along yō' hot co'n,
Bring along yō' col' co'n;
But I say bring along,
Bring along yō' * Jimmy-
john.

Some loves de hot co'n,
Some loves de col' co'n;
But I loves, I loves,
I loves dat Jimmy-john.

THE LITTLE ROOSTER

I HAD a liddle rooster,
He crowed befō' day.
'Long come a big owl,
'An toted him away.

But de rooster fight hard,
An' de owl let him go.
Now all de pretty hens
Wants dat rooster fer deir
beau.

* Jimmy-john = a whiskey jug.

SUGAR IN COFFEE

SHEEP'S in de meader a-mowin' o' de hay.
De honey's in de bee-gum, so dey all say.
My head's up an' I'se boun' to go.
Who'll take sugar in de coffee-o?

I'se de prettiest liddle gal in de county-o.
My mammy an' daddy, dey bofe say so.
I looks in de glass, it don't say, "No";
So I'll take sugar in de coffee-o.

* THE TURTLE'S SONG

MUD turkle settin' on de end of a log,
A-watchin' of a tadpole a-turnin' to a frog.
He sees Br'er B'ar a-pullin' lak a mule.
He sees Br'er Tearpin a-makin' him a fool.

Br'er B'ar pull de rope an' he puff an' he blow;
But he cain't git de Tearpin out'n de water from below.
Dat big clay root is a-holdin' dat rope,
Br'er Tearpin's got 'im fooled, an' dere hain't no hope.

* For explanation see Study in Negro Folk Rhymes.

Mud turkle settin' one de end o' dat log;
Sing fer de tadpole a-turnin' to a frog,
Sing to Br'er B'ar a-pullin' lak a mule,
Sing to Br'er Tearpin a-makin' 'im a fool:—

"Oh, Br'er Rabbit! Yō' eyes mighty big!"
"Yes, Br'er Turkle! Dey're made fer to see."
"Oh, Br'er Tearpin! Yō' house mighty cu'ous!"
"Yes, Br'er Turkle, but it jest suits me."

"Oh, Br'er B'ar! You pulls mighty stout."
"Yes, Br'er Turkle! Dat's right smart said!"
"Right, Br'er B'ar! Dat sounds bully good,
But you'd oughter git a liddle mō' pull in de head."

RACCOON AND OPOSSUM FIGHT

De raccoon an' de 'possum
Under de hill a-fightin';
Rabbit almos' bust his sides
Laughin' at de bitin'.

De raccoon claw de 'possum
Along de ribs an' head;
'Possum tumble over an' grin,
Playin' lak he been dead.

COTTON EYED JOE

Hol' my fiddle an' hol' my bow,
Whilst I knocks ole Cotton Eyed Joe.

I'd a been dead some seben years ago,
If I hadn' a danced dat Cotton Eyed
Joe.

Oh, it makes dem ladies love me so,
W'en I comes 'roun' pickin' ole
Cotton Eyed Joe!

Yes, I'd a been married some forty
year ago,
If I hadn' stay'd 'roun' wid Cotton
Eyed Joe.

I hain't seed ole Joe, since way las'
Fall;
Dey say he's been sol' down to Guinea
Gall.

RABBIT SOUP

RABBIT soup! Rabbit sop!
Rabbit e't my tunnup top.

Rabbit hop, rabbit jump,
Rabbit hide behin' dat stump.

Rabbit stop, twelve o'clock,
Killed dat rabbit wid a rock.

Rabbit's mine. Rabbit's skin'.
Dress 'im off an' take 'im in.

Rabbit's on! Dance an' whoop!
Makin' a pot o' rabbit soup!

OLD GRAY MINK

I ONCE did think dat I would sink,
But you know I wus dat ole gray mink.

Dat ole gray mink jes couldn' die,
W'en he thought about good chicken pie.

He swum dat creek above de mill,
An' he's killing an' eatin' chicken still.

RUN, NIGGER, RUN!

RUN, Nigger, run! De * Patter-rollers'll
ketch you.
Run, Nigger, run! It's almos' day.

Dat Nigger run'd, dat Nigger flew,
Dat Nigger tore his shu't in two.

All over dem woods and frou de paster,
Dem Patter-rollers shot; but de Nigger git
faster,

Oh, dat Nigger whirl'd, dat Nigger
wheel'd,
Dat Nigger tore up de whole co'n field.

SHAKE THE PERSIMMONS DOWN

DE raccoon up in de 'simmon tree.
Dat 'possum on de groun'.
De 'possum say to de raccoon:
"Suh!"
"Please shake dem 'simmons down."

* Patrollers, or white guards; on duty at night during the days of slavery; whose duty it was to see that slaves without permission to go, stayed at home.

De raccoon say to de 'possum: "Suh!"
(As he grin from down below),
"If you wants dese good 'simmons,
man,
Jes clam up whar dey grow."

THE COW NEEDS A TAIL IN FLY-TIME

DAT ole black sow, she can root in de mud,
She can tumble an' roll in de slime;
But dat big red cow, she git all mired up,
So dat cow need a tail in fly-time.

Dat ole gray hoss, wid 'is ole bob tail,
You mought buy all 'is ribs fer a dime;
But dat ole gray hoss can git a kiver on,
Whilst de cow need a tail in fly-time.

Dat Nigger Overseer, dat's a-ridin' on a
mule,
'Cain't make hisse'f white lak de lime;
Mosser mought take 'im down fer a notch
or two,
Den de cow'd need a tail in fly-time.

JAYBIRD DIED WITH THE WHOOPING COUGH

De Jaybird died wid de Whoopin' Cough,
De Sparrer died wid de colic;
'Long come de Red-bird, skippin' 'round,
Sayin': "Boys, git ready fer de Frolic!"

De Jaybird died wid de Whoopin' Cough,
De Bluebird died wid de Measles;
'Long come a Nigger wid a fiddle on his back,
'Vitin' Crows fer to dance wid de Weasels.

Dat Mockin'-bird, he romp an' sing;
Dat ole Gray Goose come prancin'.
Dat Thrasher stuff his mouf wid plums,
Den he caper on down to de dancin'.

Dey hopped it low, an' dey hopped it high;
Dey hopped it to, an' dey hopped it by;
Dey hopped it fer, an' dey hopped it nigh;
Dat fiddle an' bow jes make 'em fly.

WANTED! CORNBREAD AND COON

I'se gwine now a-huntin' to ketch a big fat coon.
Gwineter bring him home, an' bake him, an' eat him wid a spoon.
Gwineter baste him up wid gravy, an' add some onions too.
I'se gwineter shet de Niggers out, an' stuff myse'f clean through.

I wants a piece o' hoecake; I wants a piece o' bread,
An' I wants a piece o' Johnnycake as big as my ole head.
I wants a piece o' ash cake: I wants dat big fat coon!
An' I shō' won't git hongry 'fore de middle o' nex' June.

LITTLE RED HEN

My liddle red hen, wid a liddle white foot,
Done built her nes' in a huckleberry root.
She lay mō' aigs dan a flock on a fahm.
Anudder liddle drink wouldn' do us no harm.

My liddle red hen hatch fifty red chicks
In dat liddle ole nes' of huckleberry sticks.
Wid one mō' drink, ev'y chick'll make two!
Come, bring it on, Honey, an' let's git through.

RATION DAY

Dat ration dav come once a week,
Ole Mosser's rich as Gundy;
But he gives us 'lasses all de week,
An' buttermilk fer Sund'y.

Ole Mosser give me a pound o' meat.
I e't it all on Mond'y;
Den I e't 'is 'lasses all de week.
An' buttermilk fer Sund'y.

Ole Mosser give me a peck o' meal,
I fed and cotch my tucky;
But I e't dem 'lasses all de week,
An' buttermilk fer Sund'y.

Oh laugh an' sing an' don't git tired.
We's all gwine home, some Mond'y,
To de honey ponds an' fritter trees;
An' ev'ry day'll be Sund'y.

MY FIDDLE

IF my ole fiddle wus jes in chune,
She'd bring me a dollar ev'y Friday
night in June.
W'en my ole fiddle is fixed up right,
She bring me a dollar in nearly ev'y
night.
W'en my ole fiddle begin to sing,
She make de whole plantation ring.
She bring me in a dollar an' sometime
mō'.
Hurrah fer my ole fiddle an' bow!

DIE IN THE PIG-PEN FIGHTING

DAT ole sow said to de barrer:
"I'll tell you w'at let's do:
Let's go an' git dat broad-axe
And die in de pig-pen too."

"Die in de pig-pen fightin'!
Yes, die, die in de wah!
Die in de pig-pen fightin',
Yes, die wid a bitin' jaw!"

MASTER IS SIX FEET ONE WAY

MOSSER is six foot one way, an' free foot
tudder;
An' he weigh five hunderd pound.
Britches cut so big dat dey don't suit de
tailor,
An' dey don't meet half way 'round.

Mosser's coat come back to a claw-hammer
p'int.
(Speak sof' or his Bloodhound'll bite us.)
His long white stockin's mighty clean an'
nice,
But a liddle mō' holier dan righteous.

FOX AND GEESE

BR'ER Fox wa'k out one moonshiny night,
He say to hisse'f w'at he's a gwineter do.
He say, "I'se gwineter have a good piece
o' meat,
Befō' I leaves dis townyoo.
Dis townyoo, dis townyoo!
Yes, befō' I leaves dis townyoo!"

Ole mammy Sopentater jump up out'n bed,
An' she poke her head outside o' de dō'.
She say: "Ole man, my gander's gone.
I heared 'im w'en he holler 'quinny-
quanio,'
'Quinny-quanio, quinny-quanio!'
Yes, I heared 'im w'en he holler 'quinny-
quanio.' "

GOOSEBERRY WINE

Now 'umble Uncle Steben,
I wonders whar youse gwine?
Don't never tu'n yō' back, Suh,
On dat good ole gooseberry wine!

Oh walk chalk, Ginger Blue!
Git over double trouble.
You needn' min' de wedder
So's de win' don't blow you
double.

Now!
Uncle Mack! Uncle Mack!
Did you ever see de lak?
Dat good ole sweet gooseberry
wine
Call Uncle Steben back.

I WOULD RATHER BE A NEGRO THAN A POOR WHITE MAN

My name's Ran, I wuks in de san';
But I'd druther be a Nigger dan a pō'
white man.

Gwineter hitch my oxes side by side,
An' take my gal fer a big fine ride.

Gwineter take my gal to de country
stō';
Gwineter dress her up in red calico.

You take Kate, an' I'll take Joe.
Den off we'll go to de pahty-o.

Gwineter take my gal to de Hulla-
baloo,
Whar dere hain't no * Crackers in a
mile or two.

Interlocution:

(Fiddler) "Oh, Sal! Whar's de
milk strainer cloth?"

* Names applied by Negroes to the poorer class of white people in the South.

(Banjo Picker) "Bill's got it wropped 'round his ole sore leg."
(Fiddler) "Well, take it down to de gum spring an' give it a cold water rench; I 'spizes nastness anyway. I'se got to have a clean cloth fer de milk."

He don't lak whisky but he jest drinks a can.
Honey! I'd druther be a Nigger dan a pō' white man.

I'd druther be a Nigger, an' plow ole Beck
Dan a white * Hill Billy wid his long red neck.

THE HUNTING CAMP

Sam got up one mornin'
A mighty big fros'.
Saw "A louse, in de huntin' camp
As big as any hoss!"

* Names applied by Negroes to the poorer class of white people in the South.

Sam run 'way down de mountain;
But w'en Mosser got dar,
He swore it twusn't nothin'
But a big black b'ar.

THE ARK

OLE Nora had a lots o' hands
A clearin' new ground patches.
He said he's gwineter build a Ark,
An' put tar on de hatches.

He had a sassy Mo'gan hoss
An' gobs of big fat cattle;
An' he driv' em all aboard de Ark,
W'en he hear de thunder rattle.

An' den de river riz so fas'
Dat it bust de levee railin's.
De lion got his dander up,
An' he lak to a broke de palin's.

An' on dat Ark wus daddy Ham;
No udder Nigger on dat packet.
He soon got tired o' de Barber Shop,
Caze he couln' stan' de racket.

An' den jes to amuse hisse'f,
He steamed a board an' bent it, Son.
Dat way he got a banjer up,
Fer ole Ham's de fust to make one.

Dey danced dat Ark from ēen to ēen,
Ole Nora called de Figgers.
Ole Ham, he sot an' knocked de chunes,
De happiest of de Niggers.

GRAY AND BLACK HORSES

I WENT down to de woods an' I couldn' go 'cross,
So I paid five dollars fer an ole gray hoss.
De hoss wouldn' pull, so I sōl' 'im fer a bull.
De bull wouldn' holler, so I sōl' 'im fer a dollar.
De dollar wouldn' pass, so I throwed it in de grass.
Den de grass wouldn' grow. Heigho! Heigho!

Through dat huckleberry woods I couldn' git far,
So I paid a good dollar fer an ole black mar'.
W'en I got down dar, de trees wouldn' bar;
So I had to gallop back on dat ole black mar'.
"Bookitie-bar!" Dat ole black mar'; "Bookitie-bar!" Dat ole black mar'.
Yes, she trabble so hard dat she jolt off my ha'r.

RATTLER

Go call ole Rattler from de bo'n.
Here Rattler! Here!
He'll drive de cows out'n de co'n,
Here Rattler! Here!

Rattler is my huntin' dog.
Here Rattler! Here!
He's good fer rabbit, good fer hog,
Here Rattler! Here!

He's good fer 'possum in de dew.
Here Rattler! Here!
Sometimes he gits a chicken, too.
Here Rattler! Here!

BROTHER BEN AND SISTER SAL

Ole Br'er Ben's a mighty good ole man,
He don't steal chickens lak he useter.
He went down de chicken roos' las' Friday night,
An' tuck off a dominicker rooster.

Dere's ole Sis Sal, she climbs right well,
But she cain't 'gin to climb lak she useter.
So yonder she sets a shellin' out co'n
To Mammy's ole bob-tailed rooster.

Yes, ole Sis Sal's a mighty fine ole gal,
She's shō' extra good an' clever.
She's done tuck a notion all her own,
Dat she hain't gwineter marry never.

Ole Sis Sal's got a foot so big,
Dat she cain't wear no shoes an' gaiters.
So all she want is some red calico,
An' dem big yaller yam sweet taters.

Now looky, looky here! Now looky,
looky there!
Jes looky!—Looky 'way over yonder!—
Don't you see dat ole gray goose
A-smilin' at de gander?

SIMON SLICK'S MULE

DERE wus a liddle kickin' man,
His name wus Simon Slick.
He had a mule wid cherry eyes.
Oh, how dat mule could kick!

An', Suh, w'en you go up to him,
He shet one eye an' smile;
Den 'e telegram 'is foot to you,
An' sen' you half a mile!

NOBODY LOOKING

WELL: I look dis a way, an' I look dat a way,
An' I heared a mighty rumblin'.
W'en I come to find out, 'twus dad's black sow,
A-rootin' an' a-grumblin'.

Den: I slipped away down to de big White House.
Miss Sallie, she done gone 'way.
I popped myse'f in de rockin' chear,
An' I rocked myse'f all day.

Now: I looked dis a way, an' I looked dat a way,
An' I didn' see nobody in here.
I jes run'd my head in de coffee pot,
An' I drink'd up all o' de beer.

HOECAKE

IF you wants to bake a hoecake,
To bake it good an' done;
Jes' slap it on a Nigger's heel,
An' hol' it to de sun.

Dat snake, he bake a hoecake,
An' sot de toad to mind it;
Dat toad he up an' go to sleep,
An' a lizard slip an' find it!

My mammy baked a hoecake,
As big as Alabamer.
She throwed it 'g'inst a Nigger's
head
An' it ring jes' lak a hammer.

De way you bakes a hoecake,
In de ole Virginy 'tire;
You wrops it 'round a Nigger's
heel,
An' hōl's it to de fire.

I WENT DOWN THE ROAD

I WENT down de road,
I went in a whoop;
An' I met Aunt Dinah
Wid a chicken pot o' soup.
Sing: "I went away from dar; hook-a-doo-dle, hook-a-doo-dle."
"I went away from dar; hook-a-doo-dle-doo!"
I drunk up dat soup,
An' I let her go by;
An' I tōl' her nex' time
To bring Missus' pot pie.
Sing: "Oh far'-you-well; hook-a-doo-dle, hook-a-doo-dle;
Oh far'-you-well, an' a hook-a-doo-dle-doo!"

THE OLD HEN CACKLED

DE ole hen she cackled,
An' stayed down in de bo'n.
She git fat an' sassy,
A-eatin' up de co'n.

De ole hen she cackled,
Git great long yaller laigs.
She swaller down de oats,
But I don't git no aigs.

De ole hen she cackled,
She cackled in de lot,
De nex' time she cackled,
She cackled in de pot.

I LOVE SOMEBODY

I LOVES somebody, yes, I do;
An' I wants somebody to love me too.
Wid my chyart an' oxes stan'in' 'roun',
Her pretty liddle foot needn' tetch de groun'.

I loves somebody, yes, I do,
Dat randsome, handsome, Sticka-mastew.
Wid her reddingoat an' waterfall,
She's de pretty liddle gal dat beats 'em all.

WE ARE "ALL THE GO"

Yes! We's "All-de-go," boys; we's "All-de-go."
Me an' my Lulu gal's "All-de-go."
I jes' loves my sweet pretty liddle Lulu Ann,
But de way she gits my money I cain't hardly understan'.
W'en she up an' call me "Honey!" I fergits my name is Sam,
An' I hain't got one nickel lef' to git a me a dram.

Still: We's "All-de-go," boys; we's "All-de-go."
Me an' my Lulu gal's "All-de-go."
She's always gwine a-fishin', w'en she'd oughter not to go;
An' now she's all a troubled wid de frostes an' de snow.
I tells you jes one thing dat I'se done gone an' foun':
De Nigs cain't git no livin' 'round de Cō't House steps an' town.

AUNT DINAH DRUNK

OLE Aunt Dinah, she got drunk.
She fell in de fire, an' she kicked up a
 chunk.
Dem embers got in Aunt Dinah's shoe,
An' dat black Nigger shō' got up an' flew.

I likes Aunt Dinah mighty, mighty well,
But dere's jes' one thing I hates an' 'spize:
She drinks mō' whisky dan de bigges' fool,
Den she up an' tell ten thousand lies.

Yes, I won't git drunk an' kick up a
 chunk.
 I won't git drunk an' kick up a
 chunk.
 I won't git drunk an' kick up a
 chunk,
 'Way down on de ole Plank Road.
 Oh shoo my Love! My turkle dove.
 Oh shoo my Love! My turkle dove.
 Oh shoo my Love! My turkle dove.
 'Way down on de ole Plank Road.

THE OLD WOMAN IN THE HILLS

Once: Dere wus an ole 'oman
Dat lived in de hills;
Put rocks in 'er stockin's,
An' sent 'em to mill.

Den: De ole miller swore,
By de pint o' his knife;
Dat he never had ground
up
No rocks in his life.

So: De ole 'oman said
To dat miller nex' day:
"You railly must 'scuse me,
It's de onliest way."

"I beared you made meal,
A-grindin' on stones.
I mus' 'ave beared wrong,
It mus' 'ave been bones."

A SICK WIFE

Las' Sadday night my wife tuck sick,
An' what d'you reckon ail her?
She e't a tucky gobbler's head
An' her stomach, it jes' fail her.

She squall out: "Sam, bring me some
    mint!
Make catnip up an' sage tea!"
I goes an' gits her all dem things,
But she throw 'em back right to me.

Says I: "Dear Honey! Mind nex' time!"
    "Don't eat from 'A to Izzard' "
    "I thinks you won' git sick at all,
    If you saves pō' me de gizzard."

MY WONDERFUL TRAVEL

I come down from ole Virginny,
'Twas on a Summer day;
De wedder was all frez up,
'An' I skeeted all de way!

Interlocution:

Hand my banjer down to play,
Wanter pick fer dese ladies right away;

"W'en dey went to bed,
Dey couldn' shet deir eyes,"
An' "Dey was stan'in' on deir heads,
A-pickin' up de pies."

* I WOULD NOT MARRY A BLACK GIRL

I WOULDN' marry a black gal,
I'll tell you de reason why:
When she goes to comb dat head
De naps'll 'gin to fly.

I wouldn' marry a black gal,
I'll tell you why I won't:
When she'd oughter wash her face—
Well, I'll jes say she don't.

I woudn' marry a black gal,
An' dis is why I say:
When you has her face around,
It never gits good day.

* For discussion see Study in Negro Folk Rhymes.

HARVEST SONG

Las' year wus a good crap year,
An' we raised beans an' 'maters.
We didn' make much cotton an' co'n;
But, Goodness Life, de taters!

You can plow dat ole gray hoss,
I'se gwineter plow dat mulie;
An' w'en we's geddered in de craps,
I'se gwine down to see Julie.

I hain't gwineter wo'k on de rail-
road.
I hates to wo'k on de fahm.
I jes wants to set in de cool shade,
Wid my head on my Julie's ahm.

You swing Lou, an' I'll swing Sue.
Dere hain't no diffunce 'tween dese
two.
You swing Lou, I'll swing my beau;
I'se gwineter buy my gal red calico.

YEAR OF JUBILEE

NIGGERS, has you seed ole Mosser;
(Red mustache on his face.)
A-gwine 'roun' sometime dis mawnin',
'Spectin' to leave de place?

Nigger Hands all runnin' 'way,
Looks lak we mought git free!
It mus' be now de *Kingdom Come
In de Year o' Jubilee.

Oh, yon'er comes ole Mosser
Wid his red mustache all white!
It mus' be now de Kingdom Come
Sometime to-morrer night.

Yanks locked him in de smokehouse
cellar,
De key's throwed in de well:
It shō' mus' be de Kingdom Come.
Go ring dat Nigger field-bell!

* Kingdom Come = Freedom.

SHEEP SHELL CORN

Oh: De Ram blow de ho'n an' de sheep shell co'n;
An' he sen' it to de mill by de buck-eyed Whip-poorwill.
Ole Joe's dead an' gone but his * Hant blows de ho'n;
An' his hound howls still from de top o' dat hill.

Yes: De Fish-hawk said unto Mistah Crane;
"I wishes to de Lawd dat you'd sen' a liddle rain;
Fer de water's all muddy, an de creek's gone dry;
If it 'twasn't fer de tadpoles we'd all die."

Oh: When de sheep shell co'n wid de rattle of his ho'n
I wishes to de Lawd I'd never been bo'n;
Caze when de Hant blows de ho'n, de sperits all dance,
An' de hosses an' de cattle, dey whirls 'round an' prance.

* Hant = spirit or ghost.

Oh: Yonder comes Skillet an' dere goes Pot;
An' here comes Jawbone 'cross de lot.
Walk Jawbone! Beat de Skillet an' de Pan!
You cut dat Pigeon's Wing, Black Man!

Now: Take keer, gemmuns, an' let me through
Caze I'se gwineter dance wid liddle Mollie Lou.
But I'se never seed de lak since I'se been bo'n,
When de sheep shell co'n wid de rattle of his ho'n!

PLASTER

CHILLUNS:

Mammy an' daddy had a hoss,
Dey want a liddle bigger.
Dey sticked a plaster on his back
An' drawed a liddle Nigger.

Den:

Mammy an' daddy had a dog,
His tail wus short an' chunky.
Dey slapped a plaster 'round dat tail,
An' drawed it lak de monkey.

Well:

Mammy an' daddy's dead an' gone.
Did you ever hear deir story?
Dey sticked some plasters on deir heels,
An' drawed 'em up to Glory!

UNCLE NED

JES lay down de shovel an' de hoe.
Jes hang up de fiddle an' de bow.
No more hard work fer ole man Ned,
Fer he's gone whar de good Niggers go.

He didn' have no years fer to hear,
Didn' have no eyes fer to see,
Didn' have no teeth fer to eat corn cake,
An' he had to let de beefsteak be.

Dey called 'im "Ole Uncle Ned,"
A long, long time ago.
Dere wusn't no wool on de top o' his head
In de place whar de wool oughter grow.

When ole man Ned wus dead,
Mosser's tears run down lak rain;
But ole Miss, she wus a liddle sorter glad,
Dat she wouldn' see de ole Nigger 'gain.

THE MASTER'S "STOLEN" COAT

OLE Mosser bought a brand new coat,
He hung it on de wall.
Dat Nigger * stole dat coat away,
An' wore it to de Ball.

His head look lak a Coffee pot,
His nose look lak de spout,
His mouf look lak de fier place,
Wid de ashes all tuck out.

His face look lak a skillet lid,
His years lak two big kites.
His eyes look lak two big biled aigs,
Wid de yallers in de whites.

His body 'us lak a stuffed toad frog,
His foot look lak a board.
Oh-oh! He thinks he is so fine,
But he's greener dan a gourd.

* Stole, here, means taken temporarily with intention to return.

* I WOULDN'T MARRY A YELLOW OR A WHITE NEGRO GIRL

I SHO' loves dat gal dat dey calls Sally † "Black,"
An' I sorter loves some of de res';
I first loves de gals fer lovin' me,
Den I loves myse'f de bes'.

I wouldn' marry dat yaller Nigger gal,
An' I'll tell you de reason why:
Her neck's drawed out so stringy an' long,
I'se afeared she 'ould never die.

I wouldn' marry dat White Nigger gal,
(Fer gracious sakes!) dis is why:
Her nose look lak a kittle spout;
An' her skin, it hain't never dry.

DON'T ASK ME QUESTIONS

DON'T ax me no questions,
An' I won't tell you no lies;
But bring me dem apples,
An' I'll make you some pies.

* For discussion see Study in Negro Folk Rhymes.

† "Black" here is not the real name. This name is applied because of the complexion of the girls to whom it was sung.

An' if you ax questions,
'Bout my havin' de flour;
I fergits to use 'lasses
An' de pie'll be all sour.

Dem apples jes wa'k here;
An' dem 'lasses, dey run.
Hain't no place lak my house
Found un'er de sun.

THE OLD SECTION BOSS

I ONCE knowed an ole Sexion Boss but he done been laid low.
I once knowed an ole Sexion Boss but he done been laid low.
He "Caame frum gude ole Ireland some fawhrty year ago."

W'en I ax 'im fer a job, he say: "Nayger, w'at can yer do?"
W'en I ax 'im fer a job, he say: "Nayger, w'at can yer do?"
"I can line de track; tote de jack, de pick an' shovel too."

Says he: 'Nayger, de railroad's done, an' de chyars is on de track,"
Says he: "Nayger, de railroad's done, an' de chyars is on de track,"
"Transportation brung yer here, but yō' money'll take yer back."

I went down to de Deepo, an' my ticket I shō' did draw.
I went down to de Deepo, an' my ticket I shō' did draw.
To take me over dat ole Iron Mountain to de State o' Arkansaw.

As I went sailin' down de road, I met my mudder-in-law.
I wus so tired an' hongry, man, dat I couldn' wuk my jaw.
Fer I hadn't had no decent grub since I lef' ole Arkansaw.

Her bread wus hard corndodgers; dat meat, I couldn' chaw.
Her bread wus hard corndodgers; dat meat, I couldn' chaw.
You see; dat's de way de Hoosiers feeds way out in Arkansaw.

THE NEGRO AND THE POLICEMAN

"Oh Mistah Policeman, tu'n me loose;
Hain't got no money but a good excuse."
Oh hello, Sarah Jane!

Dat ole Policeman treat me mean,
He make me wa'k to Bowlin' Green.
Oh hello, Sarah Jane!

De way he treat me wus a shame.
He make me wear dat Ball an' Chain.
Oh hello, Sarah Jane!

I runs to de river, I can't git 'cross;
Dat Police grab me an' swim lak a hoss.
Oh hello, Sarah Jane!

I goes up town to git me a gun,
Dat ole Police shō' make me run.
Oh hello, Sarah Jane!

I goes crosstown sorter walkin' wid a hump
An' dat ole Police sho' make me jump.
Oh hello, Sarah Jane!

Sarah Jane, is dat yō' name?
Us boys, we calls you Sarah Jane.
Well, hello, Sarah Jane!

HAM BEATS ALL MEAT

DEM white folks set up in a Dinin' Room
An' dey charve dat mutton an' lam'.
De Nigger, he set 'hind de kitchen door,
An' he eat up de good sweet ham.

Dem white folks, dey set up an' look so fine,
An' dey eats dat ole cow meat;
But de Nigger grin an' he don't say much,
Still he know how to git what's sweet.

Deir ginger cakes taste right good sometimes,
An' deir Cobblers an' deir jam.
But fer every day an' Sunday too,
Jest gimme de good sweet ham.

Ham beats all meat,
Always good an' sweet.
Ham beats all meat,
I'se always ready to eat.
You can bake it, bile it, fry it, stew it,
An' still it's de good sweet ham.

SUZE ANN

YES: I loves dat gal wid a blue dress on,
Dat de white folks calls Suze Ann.
She's jes' dat gal what stole my heart,
'Way down in Alabam'.

But: She loves a Nigger about nineteen,
Wid his lips all painted red;
Wid a liddle fuz around his mouf;
An' no brains in his head.

Now: Looky, looky Eas'! Oh, looky, looky Wes'!
I'se been down to ole Lou'zan';
Still dat ar gal I loves de bes'
Is de gal what's named Suze Ann.
Oh, head 'er! Head 'er! Ketch 'er!
Jump up an' * "Jubal Jew."
Fer de Banger Picker's sayin':
He hain't got nothin' to do.

WALK TOM WILSON

OLE Tom Wilson, he had 'im a hoss;
His legs so long he couldn' git 'em 'cross.

* Jubal Jew is a kind of dance step.

He laid up dar lak a bag o' meal,
An' he spur him in de flank wid his toenail heel.

Ole Tom Wilson, he come an' he go,
Frum cabin to cabin in de county-o.
W'en he go to bed, his legs hang do'n,
An' his foots makes poles fer de chickens t' roost on.

Tom went down to de river, an' he couldn' go 'cross.
Tom tromp on a 'gater an' 'e think 'e wus a hoss.
Wid a mouf wide open, 'gater jump from de san',
An' dat Nigger look clean down to de Promus' Lan'.

Wa'k Tom Wilson, git out'n de way!
Wa'k Tom Wilson, don't wait all de day!
Wa'k Tom Wilson, here afternoon;
Sweep dat kitchen wid a bran' new broom.

CHICKEN PIE

If you wants to make an ole Nigger feel good,
Let me tell you w'at to do:
Jes take off a chicken from dat chicken roost,
An' take 'im along wid you.
Take a liddle dough to roll 'im up in,
An' it'll make you wink yō' eye;
W'en dat good smell gits up yō' nose,
Frum dat home-made chicken pie.

Jes go round w'en de night's sorter dark,
An' dem chickens, dey can't see.
Be shore dat de bad dog's all tied up,
Den slip right close to de tree.
Now retch out yo' han' an' pull 'im in,
Den run lak a William goat;
An' if he holler, squeeze 'is neck,
An' shove 'im un'er yō' coat.

Bake dat Chicken pie!
It's mighty hard to wait
When you see dat Chicken pie,
Hot, smokin' on de plate.
Bake dat Chicken pie!
Yes, put in lots o' spice.
Oh, how I hopes to Goodness
Dat I gits de bigges' slice.

I AM NOT GOING TO HOBO ANY MORE

My mammy done tol' me a long time ago
To always try fer to be a good boy;
To lay on my pallet an' to waller on de flō';
An' to never leave my daddy's house.
I hain't never gwineter hobo no mō'. By George!
I hain't never gwineter hobo no mō'.

Yes, befō' I'd live dat ar hobo life,
I'll tell you what I'd jes go an' do:
I'd court dat pretty gal an' take 'er fer my wife,
Den jes lay 'side dat ar hobo life.
I hain't never gwineter hobo no mō'. By George!
I hain't never gwineter hobo no mō'.

FORTY-FOUR

If de people'll jes gimme
Des a liddle bit o' peace,
I'll tell 'em what happen
To de Chief o' Perlice.
He met a robber
Right at de dō'!
An' de robber, he shot 'im
Wid a forty-fō'!
He shot dat Perliceman.
He shot 'im shō'!
What did he shoot 'im wid?
A forty-fō'.

Dey sent fer de Doctah
An' de Doctah he come.
He come in a hurry,
He come in a run.

He come wid his instriments
Right in his han',
To progue an' find
Dat forty-fō', Man!
De Doctah he progued;
He progued 'im shō'!
But he jes couldn' find
Dat forty-fō'.

Dey sent fer de Preachah,
An' de preachah he come.
He come in a walk,
An' he come in to talk.
He come wid 'is Bible,
Right in 'is han',
An' he read from dat chapter,
Forty-fō', Man!
Dat Preachah, he read.
He read, I know.
What Chapter did he read frum?
'Twus Forty-fō'!

Play Rhyme Section

BLINDFOLD PLAY CHANT

Oh blin' man! Oh blin' man!
You cain't never see.
Just tu'n 'round three times
You cain't ketch me.

Oh tu'n Eas'! Oh tu'n Wes'!
Ketch us if you can.
Did you thought dat you'd cotch us,
Mistah blin' man?

FOX AND GEESE PLAY

* (Fox *Call*) 'Fox in de mawnin'!"
(Goose *Sponse*) "Goose in de evenin'!"
(Fox *Call*) "How many geese you got?"
(Goose *Sponse*) "More 'an you're able to ketch!"

* For explanation of "call," and "sponse," see Study in Negro Folk Rhymes.

HAWK AND CHICKENS PLAY

* (CHICKEN'S *Call*) "Chickamee," chickamee, cranic-crow."
I went to de well to wash my toe.
W'en I come back, my chicken wus gone.
W'at time, ole Witch?

(Hawk *Sponse*) 'One'"
(Hawk *Call*) "I wants a chick."
(Chicken's *Sponse*) "Well, you cain't git mine."
(Hawk *Call*) "I shall have a chick!"
(Chicken's *Sponse*) "You shan't have a chick!"

CAUGHT BY THE WITCH PLAY

(HUMAN *Call*) "Molly, Molly, Molly-bright!"
(Witch *Sponse*) "Three scō' an' ten!"
(Human *Call*) "Can we git dar 'fore candle-light?"
(Witch *Sponse*) "Yes, if yō' legs is long an' light."
(Conscience's Warning *Call*) "You'd better watch out,
Or de witches'll git yer!"

* For explanation of "call," and "sponse," see Study in Negro Folk Rhymes.

* GOOSIE-GANDER PLAY RHYME

"Goosie, goosie, goosie-gander!
What d'you say?"—"Say: 'Goose!' "—
"Ve'y well, go right along, Honey!
I tu'ns yō' years a-loose."

"Goosie, goosie, goosie-gander!
What d'you say?"—"Say: 'Gander' "
"Ve'y well. Come in de ring, Honey!
I'll pull yō' years way yander!"

HAWK AND BUZZARD

Once: De Hawk an' de buzzard went to roost,
An' de hawk got up wid a broke off tooth.

Den: De hawk an' de buzzard went to law,
An' de hawk come back wid a broke up jaw.

But lastly: Dat buzzard tried to plead his case,
Den he went home wid a smashed in face.

* For explanation read the Study in Negro Folk Rhymes.

LIKES AND DISLIKES

I SHO' loves Miss Donie! Oh, yes, I do!
She's neat in de waist,
Lak a needle in de case;
An' she suits my taste.

I'se gwineter run wid Mollie Roalin'! Oh, yes, I will!
She's pretty an' nice
Lak a bottle full o' spice,
But she's done drap me twice.

I don't lak Miss Jane! Oh no, I don't.
She's fat an' stout,
Got her mouf sticked out,
An' she laks to pout.

SUSIE GIRL

RING 'round, Miss Susie gal,
Ring 'round, "My Dovie.'
Ring 'round, Miss Susie gal.
Bless you! "My Lovie."

Back 'way, Miss Susie gal.
Back 'way, "My Money."
Now come back, Miss Susie gal.
Dat's right! "My Honey."

Swing me, Miss Susie gal.
Swing me, "My Starlin'."
Jes swing me, my Susie gal.
Yes "Love!" "My Darlin'."

SUSAN JANE

I KNOW somebody's got my Lover;
Susan Jane! Susan Jane!
Oh, cain't you tell me; help me find 'er?
Susan Jane! Susan Jane!

If I lives to see nex' Fall;
Susan Jane! Susan Jane!
I hain't gwineter sow no wheat at all.
Susan Jane! Susan Jane!

'Way down yon'er in de middle o' de branch,
Susan Jane! Susan Jane!
De ole cow pat an' de buzzards dance.
Susan Jane! Susan Jane!

PEEP SQUIRREL

PEEP squir'l, ying-ding-did-lum;
Peep squir'l, it's almos' day,
Look squir'l, ying-ding-did-lum,
Look squir'l, an' run away.

Walk squir'l, ying-ding-did-lum;
Walk squir'l, fer dat's de way.
Skip squir'l, ying-ding-did-lum;
Skip squir'l, all dress in gray.

Run squir'l! Ying-ding-did-lum!
Run squir'l! Oh, run away!
I cotch you squir'l! Ying-ding-did-lum!
I cotch you squir'l! Now stay, I say.

DID YOU FEED MY COW?

"DID yer feed my cow?" Yes, Mam!"
"Will yer tell me how?" "Yes, Mam!"
"Oh, w'at did yer give 'er?" "Cawn an' hay."
"Oh, w'at did yer give 'er?" "Cawn an' hay."

"Did yer milk 'er good?" "Yes, Mam!"
"Did yer do lak yer should?" "Yes, Mam!"
"Oh, how did yer milk 'er?" "Swish! Swish! Swish!"
"Oh, how did yer milk er?" "Swish! Swish! Swish!"

"Did dat cow git sick?" "Yes, Mam!"
"Wus she kivered wid tick?" "Yes, Mam!"
"Oh, how wus she sick?" "All bloated up."
"Oh, how wus she sick?" "All bloated up."

"Did dat cow die?" "Yes, Mam!"
"Wid a pain in 'er eye?" "Yes, Mam!"
"Oh, how did she die?" "Uh-! Uh-! Uh-!"
"Oh, how did she die?" "Uh-! Uh-! Uh-!"

"Did de Buzzards come?" "Yes, Mam!"
"Fer to pick 'er bone?" "Yes, Mam!"
"Oh, how did they come?" "Flop! Flop! Flop!"
"Oh, how did they come?" "Flop! Flop! Flop!"

A BUDGET

If I lives to see nex' Spring
I'se gwineter buy my wife a big gold ring.

If I lives to see nex' Fall,
I'se gwinter buy my wife a waterfall.

"When Christmas comes?" You cunnin' elf!
I'se gwineter spen' my money on myself.

THE OLD BLACK GNATS

Dem ole black gnats, dey is so bad
I cain't git out'n here.
Dey stings, an' bites, an' runs me mad;
I cain't git out'n here.

Dem ole black gnats dey sings de song,
"You cain't git out'n here.
Ole Satan'll git you befō' long;
You cain't git out'n here."

Dey burns my years, gits in my eye;
An' I cain't git out'n here.
Dey makes me dance, dey makes me cry;
An' I cain't git out'n here.

I fans an' knocks but dey won't go 'way!
I cain't git out'n here.
Dey makes me wish 'twus Jedgment Day;
Fer I cain't git out'n here.

SUGAR LOAF TEA

Bring through yō' * Sugar-lō'-tea, bring through yō' * Candy,
All I want is to wheel, an' tu'n, an' bow to my Love so handy.

You tu'n here on Sugar-lō'-tea, I'll tu'n there on Candy.
All I want is to wheel, an' tu'n, an' bow to my Love so handy.

Some gits drunk on Sugar-lō'-tea, some gits drunk on Candy,
But all I wants is to wheel, an' tu'n, an' bow to my Love so handy.

GREEN OAK TREE! ROCKY'O

Green oak tree! Rocky'o! Green oak tree! Rocky'o!
Call dat one you loves, who it may be,
To come an' set by de side o' me.
"Will you hug 'im once an' kiss 'im twice?"
"W'y! I wouldn' kiss 'im once fer to save 'is life!"
Green oak tree! Rocky'o! Green oak tree! Rocky'o!

* Nicknames applied in imagination to the women engaged in playing in the Play Song.

KISSING SONG

A SLEISH o' bread an' butter fried,
Is good enough fer yō' sweet Bride.
Now choose yō' Lover, w'ile we sing,
An' call 'er nex' onto de ring.

"Oh my Love, how I loves you!
Nothin' 's in dis worl' above you.
Dis right han', fersake it never.
Dis heart, you mus' keep forever.
One sweet kiss, I now takes from you;
Caze I'se gwine away to leave you."

KNEEL ON THIS CARPET

JES choose yō' Eas'; jes choose yō' Wes'.
Now choose de one you loves de bes'.
If she hain't here to take 'er part
Choose some one else wid all yō' heart.

Down on dis chyarpet you mus' kneel,
Shore as de grass grows in de fiel'.
Salute yō' Bride, an' kiss her sweet,
An' den rise up upon yō' feet.

SALT RISING BREAD

I LOVES saltin', saltin' bread.
I loves saltin', saltin' bread.
Put on dat skillet, nev' mind de lead;
Caze I'se gwineter cook dat saltin' bread;
Yes, ever since my mammy's been dead,
I'se been makin' an' cookin' dat saltin' bread.

I loves saltin', saltin' bread.
I loves saltin', saltin' bread.
You loves biscuit, butter, an' fat?
I can dance Shiloh better 'an dat.
Does you turn 'round an' shake yō' head?—
Well; I loves saltin', saltin' bread.

I loves saltin', saltin' bread.
I loves saltin', saltin' bread.
W'en you ax yō' mammy fer butter an' bread,
She don't give nothin' but a stick across yō' head.
On cracklin's, you say, you wants to git fed?
Well, I loves saltin', saltin' bread.

PRECIOUS THINGS

HOL' my rooster, hōl' my hen,
Pray don't tetch my * Gooshen Ben'.

Hol' my bonnet, hōl' my shawl,
Pray don't tetch my waterfall.

Hōl' my han's by de finger tips,
But pray don't tetch my sweet liddle lips.

HE LOVES SUGAR AND TEA

MISTAH BUSTER, he loves sugar an' tea.
Mistah Buster, he loves candy.
Mistah Buster, he's a Jim-dandy!
He can swing dem gals so handy.

Charlie's up an' Charlie's down.
Charlie's fine an' dandy.
Ev'ry time he goes to town,
He gits dem gals stick candy.

Dat Niggah, he love sugar an' tea.
Dat Niggah love dat candy.

* Grecian Bend.

Fine Niggah! He can wheel 'em 'round,
An' swing dem ladies handy.

Mistah Sambo, he love sugar an' tea.
Mistah Sambo love his candy.
Mistah Sambo; he's dat han'some man
What goes wid sister Mandy.

HERE COMES A YOUNG MAN COURTING

HERE comes a young man a courtin'! Courtin'! Courtin'!
Here comes a young man a-courtin'! It's Tidlum Tidelum Day.
"Say! Won't you have one o' us? Us, Sir? Us, Sir?
Say! Won't you have one o' us, Sir?" dem brown skin ladies say.

"You is too black an' rusty! Rusty! Rusty!
You is too black an' rusty!" said Tidlum Tidelum Day.
"We hain't no blacker 'an you, Sir! You, Sir! You, Sir!
We hain't no blacker 'an you, Sir!" dem brown skin ladies say.

"Pray! Won't you have one o' us, Sir? Us, Sir? Us, Sir?
Pray! Won't you have one o' us, Sir?" say yaller gals all gay.
"You is too ragged an' dirty! Dirty! Dirty!
You is too ragged an' dirty!" said Tidlum Tidelum Day.

"You shore is got de bighead! Bighead! Bighead!
You shore is got de bighead! You needn' come dis way.
We's good enough fer you, Sir! You, Sir! You, Sir!
We's good enough fer you, Sir!" dem yaller gals all say.

"De fairest one dat I can see, dat I can see, dat I can see,
De fairest one dat I can see," said Tidlum Tidelum Day.
"My Lulu, come an' wa'k wid me, wa'k wid me, wa'k wid me.
My Lulu, come an' wa'k wid me. 'Miss Tidlum Tidelum Day.' "

ANCHOR LINE

I'SE gwine out on de Anchor Line, Dinah!
I won't git back 'fore de summer time, Dinah!
W'en I come back be "dead in line,"
I'se gwineter bring you a dollar an' a dime,
Shore as I gits in from de Anchor Line, Dinah!

If you loves me lak I loves you, Dinah!
No Coon can cut our love in two, Dinah!
If you'll jes come an' go wid me,
Come go wid me to Tennessee,
Come go wid me; I'll set you free,—Dinah!

SALLIE

SALLIE! Sallie! don't you want to marry?
Sallie! Sallie! do come an' tarry!
Sallie! Sallie! Mammy says to tell her when.
Sallie! Sallie! She's gwineter kill dat turkey hen!

Sallie! Sallie! When you goes to marry,
(Sallie! Sallie!) Marry a fahmin man(!)
(Sallie Sallie!) Ev'ry day'll be Mond'y,
(Sallie! Sallie!) Wid a hoe-handle in yō' han'!

* SONG TO THE RUNAWAY SLAVE

Go 'way from dat window, "My Honey, My Love!"
Go 'way from dat window! I say.
De baby's in de bed, an' his mammy's lyin' by,
But you cain't git yō' lodgin' here.

Go 'way from dat window, "My Honey, My Love!"
Go 'way from dat window! I say;
Fer ole Mosser's got 'is gun, an' to Miss'ip' youse been sōl';
So you cain't git yō' lodgin' here.

Go 'way from dat window, 'My Honey, My Love!"
Go 'way from dat window! I say.

* The story went among Negroes that a runaway slave husband returned every night, and knocked on the window of his wife's cabin to get food. Other slaves having betrayed the secret that he was still in the vicinity, he was sold in the woods to a slave trader at reduced price. This trader was to come next day with bloodhounds to hunt him down. On the night after the sale, when the runaway slave husband knocked, the slave wife pinched their baby to make it cry. Then she sang the above song (as if singing to the baby), so that he might, if possible, effect his escape.

De baby keeps a-cryin'; but you'd better un'erstan'
Dat you cain't git yō' lodgin' here.

Go 'way from dat window, "My Honey, My Love!"
Go 'way from dat window! I say;
Fer de Devil's in dat man, an' you'd better un'erstan'
Dat you cain't git yō' lodgin' here.

DOWN IN THE LONESOME GARDEN

HAIN'T no use to weep, hain't no use to moan;
Down in a lonesome gyardin.
You cain't git no meat widout pickin' up a bone,
Down in a lonesome gyardin.

Look at dat gal! How she puts on airs,
Down in de lonesome gyardin!
But whar did she git dem closes she w'ars,
Down in de lonesome gyardin?

It hain't gwineter rain, an' it hain't gwineter snow;
Down in my lonesome gyardin.
You hain't gwinter eat in my kitchen doo',
Nor down in my lonesome gyardin.

LITTLE SISTER, WON'T YOU MARRY ME?

Liddle sistah in de barn, jine de weddin'.
Youse de sweetest liddle couple dat I ever did see.
Oh Love! Love! Ahms all 'round me!
Say, liddle sistah, won't you marry me?

Oh step back, gal, an' don't you come a nigh me,
Wid all dem sassy words dat you say to me.
Oh Love! Love! Abms all 'roun' me!
Oh liddle sistah, won't you marry me?

RAISE A "RUCUS" TO-NIGHT

Two liddle Niggers all dressed in white, (Raise a rucus to-night.)
Want to go to Heaben on de tail of a kite. (Raise a rucus to-night.)
De kite string broke; dem Niggers fell; (Raise a rucus to-night.)
Whar dem Niggers go, I hain't gwineter tell. (Raise a rucus to-night.)

A Nigger an' a w'ite man a playin' seben up;
(Raise a rucus to-night.)
De Nigger beat de w'ite man, but 'ē's skeered to pick it up. (Raise a rucus to-night.)
Dat Nigger grabbed de money, an' de w'ite man fell.
(Raise a rucus to-night.)
How de Nigger run, I'se not gwineter tell. (Raise a rucus to-night.)

Look here, Nigger! Let me tell you a naked fac':
(Raise a rucus to-night.)
You mought a been cullud widout bein' dat black;
(Raise a rucus to-night.)
Dem 'ar feet look lak youse shō' walkin' back;
(Raise a rucus to-night.)
An' yō' ha'r, it look lak a chyarpet tack. (Raise a rucus to-night.)

Oh come 'long, chilluns, come 'long,
W'ile dat moon are shinin' bright.
Let's git on board, an' float down de river,
An' raise dat rucus to-night.

SWEET PINKS AND ROSES

Sweet pinks an' roses, strawbeers on de vines,
Call in de one you loves, an' kiss 'er if you minds.
Here sets a pretty gal,
Here sets a pretty boy;
Cheeks painted rosy, an' deir eyes battin' black.
You kiss dat pretty gal, an' I'll stan' back.

Pastime Rhyme Section

SATAN

De Lawd made man, an' de man made money.
De Lawd made de bees, an' de bees made honey.
De Lawd made ole Satan, an' ole Satan he make sin.
Den de Lawd, He make a liddle hole to put ole Satan in.

Did you ever see de Devil, wid his iron handled shovel,
A scrapin' up de san' in his ole tin pan?
He cuts up mighty funny, he steals all yō' money,
He blinds you wid his san'. He's tryin' to git you, man!

JOHNNY BIGFOOT

Johnny, Johnny Bigfoot!
Want a pair o' shoes?
Go kick two cows out'n deir skins.
Run Brudder, tell de news!

THE THRIFTY SLAVE

Jes wuk all day,
Den go huntin' in de wood.
Ef you cain't ketch nothin',
Den you hain't no good.
Don't look at Mosser's chickens,
Caze dey're roostin' high.
Big pig, liddle pig, root hog or die!

WILD NEGRO BILL

I'se wild Nigger Bill
Frum Redpepper Hill.
I never did wo'k, an' I never will.

I'se done killed de Boss.
I'se knocked down de hoss.
I eats up raw goose widout apple sauce!

I'se Run-a-way Bill,
I knows dey mought kill;
But ole Mosser hain't cotch me, an' he never
will!

YOU LOVE YOUR GIRL

You loves yō' gal?
Well, I loves mine.
Yō' gal hain't common?
Well, my gal's fine.

I loves my gal,
She hain't no goose—
Blacker 'an blackberries,
Sweeter 'an juice.

FRIGHTENED AWAY FROM A CHICKEN-ROOST

I WENT down to de hen house on my knees,
An' I thought I beared dat chicken sneeze.
You'd oughter seed dis Nigger a-gittin' 'way frum
dere,
But 'twusn't nothin' but a rooster sayin' his prayer.
How I wish dat rooster's prayer would en',
Den perhaps I mought eat dat ole gray hen.

BEDBUG

De June-bug's got de golden wing,
De Lightning-bug de flame;
De Bedbug's got no wing at all,
But he gits dar jes de same.

De Punkin-bug's got a punkin smell,
De Squash-bug smells de wust;
But de puffume of dat ole Bedbug,
It's enough to make you bust.

W'en dat Bedbug come down to my house,
I wants my walkin' cane.
Go git a pot an' scald 'im hot!
Good-by, Miss Lize Jane!

HOW TO GET TO GLORY LAND

If you wants to git to Glory Land,
I'll tell you what to do:
Jes grease yō' heels wid mutton sue,
W'en de Devil's atter you.
Jes grease yō' heel an' grease yō' han',
An' slip 'way—over into Glory Lan'.

DESTITUTE FORMER SLAVE OWNERS

Missus an' Mosser a-walkin' de street,
Deir han's in deir pockets an' nothin' to eat.
She'd better be home a-washin' up de dishes,
An' a-cleanin' up de ole man's raggitty britches.
He'd better run 'long an' git out de hoes
An' clear out his own crooked weedy corn rows;
De Kingdom is come, de Niggers is free.
Hain't no Nigger slaves in de Year Jubilee.

FATTENING FROGS FOR SNAKES

You needn' sen' my gal hoss apples,
You needn' sen' her 'lasses candy;
She would keer fer de lak o' you,
Ef you'd sen' her apple brandy.

W'y don't you git some common sense?
Jes git a liddle! Oh fer land sakes!
Quit yō' foolin', she hain't studyin' you!
Youse jes fattenin' frogs fer snakes!

THE MULE'S KICK

Is dis me, or not me,
Or is de Devil got me?
Wus dat a muskit shot me?
Is I laid here more'n a week?—
Dat ole mule do kick amazin',
An' I 'spec's he's now a-grazin'
On de t'other side de creek.

CHRISTMAS TURKEY

I PRAYED to de Lawd fer tucky-o.
Dat tucky wouldn' come.
I prayed, an' I prayed 'til I'se almos' daid.
No tucky at my home.

Chrismus Day, she almos' here;
My wife, she mighty mad.
She want dat tucky mo' an' mo'.
An' she want 'im mighty bad.

I prayed 'til de scales come on my knees,
An' still no tucky come.
I tuck myse'f to my tucky roos',
An' I brung my tucky home.

A FULL POCKETBOOK

De goose at de barn, he feel mighty funny,
Caze de duck find a pocketbook chug full o' money.
De goose say: "Whar is you gwine, my Sonny?"
An' de duck, he say: "Now good-by, Honey."

De duck chaw terbacker an' de goose drink wine,
Wid a stuffed pocketbook dey shō' had a good time;
De grasshopper played de fiddle on a punkin vine
'Till dey all fall over on a sorter dead line.

NO ROOM TO POKE FUN

Nev' mīn' if my nose are flat,
An' my face are black an' sooty;
De Jaybird hain't so big in song,
An' de Bullfrog hain't no beauty.

CROOKED NOSE JANE

I courted a gal down de lane.
Her name, it wus Crooked Nose Jane.
Her face wus white speckled, her lips wus all red,
An' she look jes as lean as a weasel half-fed.

BAD FEATURES

Blue gums an' black eyes;
Run 'round an' tell lies.
Liddle head, liddle wit;
Big long head, not a bit.

Wid his long crooked toes,
An' his heel right roun';
Dat flat-footed Nigger
Make a hole in de groun'.

MISS SLIPPY SLOPPY

Ole Miss Slippy Sloppy jump up out'n bed,
Den out'n de winder she poke 'er nappy head,
"Jack! O Jack! De gray goose's dead.
Dat fox done gone an' bit off 'er head!"

Jack run up de hill an' he call Mosser's hounds;
An' w'en dat fox hear dem turble sounds,
He sw'ar by his head an' his hide all 'round,
Dat he don't want no dinner, but a hole in de ground.

HOW TO MAKE IT RAIN

Go kill dat snake an' hang him high,
Den tu'n his belly to de sky.
De storm an' rain'll come bye an' bye.

A WIND-BAG

A NIGGER come a-struttin' up to me las' night;
In his han' wus a walkin' cane,
He tipped his hat an' give a low bow;
"Howdy-doo! Miss Lize Jane!"

But I didn' ax him how he done,
Which make a hint good pinned,
Dat I'd druther have a paper bag,
When it's sumpin' to be filled up wid wind.

GOING TO BE GOOD SLAVES

OLE Mosser an' Missus has gone down to town,
Dey said dey'd git us somethin' an' dat hain't no
jokes.
I'se gwineter be good all de whilst dey're all 'way,
An' I'se gwineter wear stockin's jes lak de white
folks.

*PAGE'S GEESE

OLE man Page'll be in a turble rage,
W'en he find out, it'll raise his dander.
Yankee soldiers bought his geese, fer one cent a-piece,
An' sent de pay home by de gander.

TO WIN A YELLOW GIRL

IF you wants to win a yaller gal,
I tell you what you do;
You "borrow" Mosser's Beaver hat,
An' slip on his Long-tailed Blue.

SEX LAUGH

YOU'SE heared a many a gal laugh,
An' say: "He! He-he! He-he-he!"
But you hain't beared no boy laugh,
An' say: "She! She-she! She-she-she!"

* The Northern soldiers during the Civil War took all of a Southern planter's geese except one lone gander. They put one penny, for each goose taken, into a small bag and tied this bag around the gander's neck. They then sent him home to his owner with the pay of one penny for each goose taken. The Negroes of the community at once made up this little song.

OUTRUNNING THE DEVIL

I WENT upon de mountain,
An' I seed de Devil comin'.
I retched an' got my hat an' coat,
An' I beat de Devil runnin'.

As I run'd down across de fiel',
A rattlesnake bit me on de heel.
I rears an' pitches an' does my bes',
An' I falls right back in a hornet's nes'.

For w'en I wus a sinnah man,
I rund by leaps an' boun's.
I wus afeard de Devil 'ould ketch me
Wid his ole three legged houn's.

But now I'se come a Christun,
I kneels right down an' prays,
An' den de Devil runs from me—
I'se tried dem other ways.

HOW TO KEEP OR KILL THE DEVIL

If you wants to see de Devil smile,
Simpully do lak his own chile.

If you wants to see de Devil git spunk,
Swallow whisky, an' git drunk.

If you wants to see de Devil live,
Cuss an' swar an' never give.

If you wants to see de Devil run,
Jes tu'n a loose de Gospel gun.

If you wants to see de Devil fall,
Hit him wid de Gospel ball.

If you wants to see de Devil beg,
Nail him wid a Gospel peg.

If you wants to see de Devil sick,
Beat him wid a Gospel stick.

If you wants to see de Devil die,
Feed him up on Gospel pie.

But de Devil w'ars dat iron shoe,
An' if you don't watch, he'll slip it on you.

JOHN HENRY

John Henry, he wus a steel-drivin' man.
He died wid his hammer in his han'.
O come long boys, an' line up de track,
For John Henry, he hain't never comin' back.

John Henry said to his Cappun: "Boss,
A man hain't nothin' but a man,
An' 'fore I'll be beat in dis sexion gang,
I'll die wid a hammer in my han'."

John Henry, he had a liddle boy,
He helt 'im in de pam of his han';
An' de las' word he say to dat chile wus:
"I wants you to be my steel-drivin' man."

John Henry, he had a pretty liddle wife,
An' her name, it wus Polly Ann.
She walk down de track, widout lookin' back,
For to see her big fine steel-drivin' man.

John Henry had dat pretty liddle wife,
An' she went all dress up in red.
She walk ev'y day down de railroad track
To de place whar her steel-drivin' man fell dead.

* THE NASHVILLE LADIES

Dem Nashville ladies dress up fine.
Got longpail hoopskirts hanging down behīn'!
Got deir bonnets to deir shoulders an' deir noses in de sky!
Big pig! Liddle pig! Root hog, or die!

THE RASCAL

I'se de bigges' rascal fer my age.
I now speaks from dis public stage.
I'se stole a cow; I'se stole a calf,
An' dat hain't more 'an jes 'bout half.

Yes, Mosser!—Lover of my soul!—
"How many chickens has I stole?"
Well; three las' night, an' two night befo';
An' I'se gwine 'fore long to git four mō'.

But you see dat hones' Billy Ben,
He done e't more dan erry three men.
He e't a ham, den e't a side;
He would a e't mō', but you know he died.

* The name of the place was used where the rhyme was repeated.

COFFEE GROWS ON WHITE FOLKS' TREES

Coffee grows on w'ite folks' trees,
But de Nigger can git dat w'en he please.
De w'ite folks loves deir milk an' brandy,
But dat black gal's sweeter dan 'lasses candy.

Coffee grows on w'ite folks trees,
An' dere's a river dat runs wid milk an' brandy.
De rocks is broke an' filled wid gold,
So dat yaller gal loves dat high-hat dandy.

AUNT JEMIMA

Ole Aunt Jemima grow so tall,
Dat she couldn' see de groun'.
She stumped her toe, an' down she fell
From de Blackwoods clean to town.

W'en Aunt Jemima git in town,
An' see dem "tony" ways,
She natchully faint an' back she fell
To de Backwoods whar she stays.

THE MULE'S NATURE

If you sees a mule tied up to a tree,
You mought pull his tail an' think about me.
For if a Nigger don't know de natcher of a mule,
It makes no diffunce what 'comes of a fool.

I'M A "ROUND-TOWN" GENTLEMAN

I hain't no wagon, hain't no dray,
Jes come to town wid a load o' hay.
I hain't no cornfield to go to bed
Wid a lot o' hay-seeds in my head.
I'se a "round-town" Gent an' I don't choose
To wuk in de mud, an' do widout shoes.

THIS SUN IS HOT

Dis sun are hot,
Dis hoe are heavy,
Dis grass grow furder dan I can reach;
An' as I looks
At dis Cotton fiel',
I thinks I mus' 'a' been called to preach.

UNCLE JERRY FANTS

Has you heared 'bout Uncle Jerry Fants?
He's got on some cu'ious shapes.
He's de one what w'ars dem white duck pants,
An' he sot down on a bunch o' grapes.

KEPT BUSY

Jes as soon as de sun go down,
My True-love's on my min'.
An' jes as soon as de daylight breaks
De white folks is got me a gwine.

She's de sweetes' thing in town;
An' when I sees dat Nig,
She make my heart go "pitty-pat,"
An' my head go "whirly-gig."

CROSSING A FOOT-LOG

Me an' my wife an' my bobtail dog
Start 'cross de creek on a hick'ry log.
We all fall in an' git good wet,
But I helt to my liddle brown jug, you bet!

WATERMELON PREFERRED

DAT hambone an' chicken are sweet.
Dat 'possum meat are sholy fine.
But give me,—now don't you cheat!—
(Oh, I jes wish you would give me!)
Dat watermillion, smilin' on de vine.

"THEY STEAL" GOSSIP

You know:

Some folks say dat a Nigger won't steal,
But Mosser cotch six in a watermillion fiel';
A-cuttin', an' a-pluggin' an' a-tearin' up de vines,
A-eatin' all de watermillions, an' a-stackin' up de rinds.

Uh-huh! Yes, I heared dat:

Ole Mosser stole a middlin' o' meat,
Ole Missus stole a ham;
Dey sent 'em bofe to de Wuk-house,
An' dey had to leave de land.

FOX AND RABBIT DRINKING PROPOSITIONS

Fox on de low ground,
Rabbit on de hill.
Says he: "I'll take a drink,
An' leave you a gill."

De fox say: "Honey,
(You sweet liddle elf!)
Jes hand me down de whole cup;
I wants it fer myself."

A TURKEY FUNERAL

Dis tucky once on earth did dwell;
An' "Gobble! Gobble! Gobble!"
But now he gives me bigges' joy,
An' rests from all his trouble.

Yes, now he's happy, so am I;
No bankerin' fer a feas':
Because I'se stuffed wid tucky meat,
An' he struts in tucky peace.

OUR OLD MULE

We had an ole mule an' he wouldn' go "gee";
So I knocked 'im down wid a single-tree.
To daddy dis wus some mighty bad news,
So he made me jump up an' outrun de Jews.

THE COLLEGE OX

Ole Ox! Ole Ox! How'd you come up here?
You'se shō' plowed de cotton fields for many a, many a year.
You'se been kicked an' cuffed about wid heaps an' heaps abuse.
Now! Now, you comes up here fer some sort o' College use.

CARE IN BREAD-MAKING

W'en you sees dat gal o' mine,
Jes tell 'er fer me, if you please,
Nex' time she goes to make up bread
To roll up 'er dirty sleeves.

WHY LOOK AT ME?

WHAT'S you lookin' at me fer?
I didn' come here to stay.
I wants dis bug put in yō' years,
An' den I'se gwine away.

I'se got milk up in my bucket,
I'se got butter up in my bowl;
But I hain't got no Sweetheart
Fer to save my soul.

A SHORT LETTER

SHE writ me a letter
As long as my eye.
An' she say in dat letter:
"My Honey!—Good-by!"

DOES MONEY TALK?

DEM whitefolks say dat money talk.
If it talk lak dey tell,
Den ev'ry time it come to Sam,
It up an' say: "Farewell!"

I'LL EAT WHEN I'M HUNGRY

I'll eat when I'se hongry,
An' I'll drink when I'se dry;
An' if de whitefolks don't kill me,
I'll live till I die.

In my liddle log cabin,
Ever since I'se been born;
Dere hain't been no nothin'
'Cept dat hard salt parch corn.

But I knows whar's a henhouse,
An' de tucky he charve;
An' if ole Mosser don't kill me,
I cain't never starve.

HEAR-SAY

Hello! Br'er Jack. How do you do?
I'se been a-hearin' a heaps o' things 'bout you.
I'll jes declar! It beats de Dickuns!
Dey's been tryin' to say you's been a-stealin' chickens!

NEGRO SOLDIER'S CIVIL WAR CHANT

OLE * Abe (God bless 'is ole soul!)
Got a plenty good victuals, an' a plenty good clo'es.
Got powder, an' shot, an' lead,
To bust in Adam's liddle Confed'
In dese hard times.

Oh, once dere wus union, an' den dere wus peace;
De slave, in de cornfield, bare up to his knees.
But de Rebel's in gray, an' Sesesh's in de way,
An' de slave'll be free
In dese hard times.

PARODY ON "NOW I LAY ME DOWN TO SLEEP"

UH-HUH: "Now I lays me down to sleep!"—
While dead oudles o' bedbugs 'round me creep,—
Well: If dey bites me befō' "I" wake,
I hopes "deir" ole jawbones'll break.

* Abraham Lincoln.

I'LL GET YOU, RABBIT!

RABBIT! Rabbit! You'se got a mighty habit,
A-runnin' through de grass,
Eatin' up my cabbages;
But I'll git you shore at las'.

Rabbit! Rabbit! Ole rabbit in de bottoms,
A-playin' in de san',
By to-morrow mornin',
You'll be in my fryin' pan.

THE ELEPHANT

MY mammy gimme fifteen cents
Fer to see dat elephan' jump de fence.
He jump so high, I didn' see why,
If she gimme a dollar he mought not cry.

So I axed my mammy to gimme a dollar,
Fer to go an' hear de elephan' holler.
He holler so loud, he skeered de crowd.

Nex' he jump so high, he tetch de sky;
An' he won't git back 'fore de fo'th o'
July.

A FEW NEGROES BY STATES

Alabammer Nigger say he love mush.
Tennessee Nigger say: ‘Good Lawd, hush!”

Fifteen cents in de panel of de fence,
South Ca'lina Nigger hain't got no sense.

Dat Kentucky Nigger jes think he's fine,
'Cause he drink dat Gooseberry wine.

I'se done heared some twenty year ago
Dat de Missippi Nigger hafter sleep on de flō'.

Lousanner Nigger fall out'n de bed,
An' break his head on a pone o' co'n bread.

HOW TO PLEASE A PREACHER

If you wants to see dat Preachah laugh,
Jes change up a dollar, an' give 'im a half.
If you wants to make dat Preachah sing,
Kill dat tucky an' give him a wing.
If you wants to see dat Preachah cry,
Kill dat chicken an' give him a thigh.

LOOKING FOR A FIGHT

I WENT down town de yudder night,
A-raisin' san' an' a-wantin' a fight.
Had a forty dollar razzer, an' a gatlin' gun,
Fer to shoot dem Niggers down one by one.

I'LL WEAR ME A COTTON DRESS

OH, will you wear red? Oh, will you wear red?
Oh, will you wear red, Milly Biggers?
"I won't wear red,
It's too much lak Missus' head.
I'll wear me a cotton dress,
Dyed wid copperse an' oak-bark."

Oh, will you wear blue? Oh, will you wear blue?
Oh, will you wear blue, Milly Biggers?
"I won't wear blue,
It's too much lak Missus' shoe.
I'll wear me a cotton dress,
Dyed wid copperse an' oak-bark."

You sholy would wear gray? You sholy would
wear gray?
You sholy would wear gray, Milly Biggers?
"I won't wear gray,
It's too much lak Missus' way.
I'll wear me a cotton dress,
Dyed wid copperse an' oak-bark."

Well, will you wear white? Well, will you wear
white?
Well, will you wear white, Milly Biggers?
"I won't wear white,
I'd get dirty long 'fore night.
I'll wear me a cotton dress,
Dyed wid copperse an' oak-bark."

Now, will you wear black? Now, will you wear
black?
Now, will you wear black, Milly Biggers?
"I mought wear black,
Case it's de color o' my back;
An' it looks lak my cotton dress,
Dyed wid * copperse an' oak-bark."

* Copperse is copperas, or sulphate of iron.

HALF WAY DOINGS

My dear Brudders an' Sisters,
As I comes here to-day,
I hain't gwineter take no scripture verse
Fer what I'se gwineter say.

My words I'se gwineter cut off short
An' I 'spects to use dis tex':
"Dis half way doin's hain't no 'count
Fer dis worl' nor de nex'."

Dis half way doin's, Brudderin,
Won't never do, I say.
Go to yō' wuk, an' git it done,
An' den's de time to play.

Fer w'en a Nigger gits lazy,
An' stops to take short naps,
De weeds an' grass is shore to grow
An' smudder out his craps.

Dis worl' dat we's a livin' in
Is sumpen lak a cotton row:
Whar each an' ev'ry one o' us
Is got his row to hoe.

An' w'en de cotton's all laid by,
De rain, it spile de bowls,
If you don't keep busy pickin'
In de cotton fiel' of yō' souls.

Keep on a-plowin', an' a-hoein';
Keep on scrapin' off de rows;
An' w'en de year is over
You can pay off all you owes.

But w'en you sees a lazy Nigger
Stop workin', shore's you're born,
You'se gwineter see him comin' out
At de liddle end of de horn.

TWO TIMES ONE

Two times one is two.
Won't you jes keep still till I gits through?
Three times three is nine.
You 'tend to yō' business, an' I'll tend to
mine.

HE PAID ME SEVEN (PARODY)

"Our Fadder, Which are in Heaben!"—
White man owe me leben and pay me seben.
"D'y Kingdom come! D'y Will be done!"—
An' if I hadn't tuck dat, I wouldn' git none.

PARODY ON "REIGN, MASTER JESUS, REIGN!"

Oh rain! Oh rain! Oh rain, "good" Mosser!
Rain, Mosser, rain! Rain hard!
Rain flour an' lard an' a big hog head
Down in my back yard.

An' w'en you comes down to my cabin,
Come down by de corn fiel'.
If you cain't bring me a piece o' meat,
Den bring me a peck o' meal.

Oh rain! Oh rain! Oh rain, "good" Mosser!
Dat good rain gives mō' rest.
"What d'you say? You Nigger, dar!"—
"Wet ground grows grass best."

A REQUEST TO SELL

GWINETER ax my daddy to sell ole Rose,
So's I can git me some new clō's.
Gwineter ax my daddy to sell ole Nat,
So's I can git a bran' new hat.
Gwineter ax my daddy to sell ole Bruise,
Den I can git some Brogran shoes.
Now, I'se gwineter fix myse'f "jes so,"
An' take myse'f down to Big Shiloh.
I'se gwine right down to Big Shiloh
To take dat t'other Nigger's beau.

WE'LL STICK TO THE HOE

WE'LL stick to de hoe, till de sun go down.
We'll rise w'en de rooster crow,
An' go to de fiel' whar de sun shine hot,
To de fiel' whar de sugar cane grow.
Yes, Chilluns, we'll all go!
We'll go to de fiel' whar de sun shine hot.
To de fiel' whar de sugar cane grow.

Oh, sing 'long boys, fer de wuk hain't hard!
Oh scrape an' clean up de row.
Fer de grass musn' grow, while de sun
shine hot,
In de fiel' whar de sugar cane grow.
No, Chilluns. No, No!
Dat grass musn' grow, while de sun shine
hot,
In de fiel' whar de sugar cane grow.

Don't think 'bout de time, fer de time
hain't long.
Yō' life soon come an' go;
Den good-bye fiel' whar de sun shine hot,
To de fiel' whar de sugar cane grow.
Yes, Chilluns. We'll all go!
Good-by to de fiel' whar de sun shine hot,
To de fiel' whar de sugar cane grow.

A FINE PLASTER

W'EN it's sheep skin an' beeswax,
It shō's a mighty fine plaster:
De mō' you tries to pull it off,
De mō' it sticks de faster.

A DAY'S HAPPINESS

FUST: I went out to milk an' I didn' know how,
I milked dat goat instid o' dat cow;
While a Nigger a-settin' wid a gapin' jaw,
Kept winkin' his eye at a tucky in de straw.

Den: I went out de gate an' I went down de road,
An' I met Miss 'Possum an' I met Mistah Toad;
An' ev'y time Miss 'Possum 'ould sing,
Mistah Toad 'ould cut dat Pigeon's Wing.

But: I went in a whoop, as I went down de road;
I had a bawky team an' a heavy load.
I cracked my whip, an' ole Beck sprung,
An' she busted out my wagin tongue.

Well: Dat night dere 'us a-gittin' up, shores you're born.
De louse go to supper, an' de flea blow de horn.
Dat raccoon paced, an' dat 'possum trot;
Dat ole goose laid, an' de gander sot.

MASTER KILLED A BIG BULL

MOSSER killed a big bull,
Missus cooked a dish full,
Didn't give poor Nigger a mouf full.
Humph! Humph!

Mosser killed a fat lam'.
Missus brung a basket,
An' give poor Nigger de haslet.
Eh-eh! Eh-eh!

Mosser killed a fat hog
Missus biled de middlin's,
An' give poor Nigger de chitlin's.
Shō! Shō!

YOU HAD BETTER MIND MASTER

'WAY down yon'er in 'Possum Trot,
(In ole Miss'sip' whar de sun shines hot)
Dere hain't no chickens an' de Niggers eats c'on;
You hain't never see'd de lak since youse been bo'n,
You'd better mīn' Mosser an' keep a stiff lip,
So's you won't git sōl' down to ole Miss'sip'.

Love Rhyme Section

PRETTY LITTLE PINK

My pretty liddle Pink,
I once did think,
Dat we-uns shō' would marry;
But I'se done give up,
Hain't got no hope,
I hain't got no time to tarry.
I'll drink coffee dat flows,
From oaks dat grows,
'Long de river dat flows wid brandy.

A BITTER LOVERS' QUARREL—ONE SIDE

You nasty dog! You dirty hog!
You thinks somebody loves you.
I tells you dis to let you know
I thinks myse'f above you.

ROSES RED

Rose's red, vi'lets blue.
Sugar is sweet but not lak you.
De vi'lets fade, de roses fall;
But you gits sweeter, all in all.

As shore as de grass grows 'round de stump,
You is my darlin' Sugar Lump.
W'en de sun don't shine de day is cold,
But my love fer you do not git old.

De ocean's deep, de sky is blue;
Sugar is sweet, an' so is you;
De ocean waves an' de sky gits pale,
But my love are true, an' it never fail.

YOU HAVE MADE ME WEEP

You'se made me weep, you'se made me mourn,
You'se made me tears an' sorrow.
So far' you well, my pretty liddle gal,
I'se gwine away to-morrow.

MOURNING SLAVE FIANCEES

Look down dat lonesome road! Look down!
De way are dark an' cōl'.
Dey makes me weep, dey makes me mourn;
All 'cause my love are sōl'.

O don't you see dat turkle dove,
What mourns from vine to vine?
She mourns lak I moans fer my love,
Lef' many a mile behin'.

DO I LOVE YOU?

Does I love you wid all my heart?—
I loves you wid my liver;
An' if I had you in my mouf,
I'd spit you in de river.

LOVERS' GOOD-NIGHT

Cotton fields white in de bright moonlight,
Now kiss yō' gal' an' say "Good-night."
If she don't kiss you, jes go on 'way;
Hain't no need a-stayin' ontel nex' day.

VINIE

I LOVES coffee, an' I loves tea.
I axes you, Vinie, does you love me?

My day's study's Vinie, an' my midnight dreams,
My apples, my peaches, my tunnups, an' greens.

Oh, I wants dat good 'possum, an' I wants to be free;
But I don't need no sugar, if Vinie love me.

De river is wide, an' I cain't well step it.
I loves you, dear Vinie; an' you know I cain't he'p it.

Dat sugar is sweet, an' dat butter is greasy;
But I loves you, sweet Vinie; don't be oneasy.

Some loves ten, an' some loves twenty,
But I loves you, Vinie, an' dat is a plenty.

Oh silver, it shine, an' lakwise do tin.
De way I loves Vinie, it mus' be a sin.

Well, de cedar is green, an' so is de pine.
God bless you, Vinie! I wish you 'us mine.

Love Song Rhyme Section

SHE HUGGED ME AND KISSED ME

I SEE'D her in de Springtime,
I see'd her in de Fall,
I see'd her in de Cotton patch,
A cameing from de Ball.

She hug me, an' she kiss me,
She wrung my han' an' cried.
She said I wus de sweetes' thing
Dat ever lived or died.

She hug me an' she kiss me.
Oh Heaben! De touch o' her han'!
She said I wus de puttiest thing
In de shape o' mortal man.

I told her dat I love her,
Dat my love wus bed-cord strong;
Den I axed her w'en she'd have me,
An' she jes say "Go long!"

IT IS HARD TO LOVE

It's hard to love, yes, indeed 'tis.
It's hard to be broke up in min'.
You'se all lugged up in some gal's heart,
But you hain't gwineter lug up in
mine.

ME AND MY LOVER

Me an' my Lover, we fall out.
How d'you reckon de fuss begun?
She laked licker, an' I laked fun,
An' dat wus de way de fuss begun.

Me an' my Lover, we fall out.
W'at d'you reckon de fuss wus 'bout?
She loved bitters, an' I loved kraut,
An' dat wus w'at de fuss wus 'bout.

Me an' my Lover git clean 'part.
How d'you reckon dat big fuss start?
She's got a gizzard, an' I'se got a heart,
An' dat's de way dat big fuss start.

I WISH I WAS AN APPLE

OH: I wish I wus an apple,
An' my Sallie wus anudder.
What a pretty match we'd be,
Hangin' on a tree togedder!

But: If I wus an apple,
An' my Sallie wus anudder;
We'd grow up high, close to de sky,
Whar de Niggers couldn' git 'er.

We'd grow up close to de sun
An' smile up dar above;
Den we'd fall down 'way in de groun'
To sleep an' dream 'bout love.

And: W'en we git through a dreamin',
We'd bofe in Heaben wake.
No Nigger shouldn' git my gal
W'en 'is time come to bake.

REJECTED BY ELIZA JANE

W'EN I went 'cross de cotton patch
I give my ho'n a blow.
I thought I beared pretty Lizie say:
"Oh, yon'er come my beau!"

So: I axed pretty Lizie to marry me,
An' what d'you reckon she said?
She said she wouldn' marry me,
If ev'ybody else wus dead.

An': As I went up de new cut road,
An' she go down de lane;
Den I thought I beared somebody
say:
"Good-bye, ole Lize Jane!"

Well: Jes git 'long, Lizie, my true love.
Git 'long, Miss Lizie Jane.
Perhaps you'll * sack "Ole Sour Bill"
An' git choked on "Sugar Cain."

* Sack = To reject as a lover.

Courtship Rhyme Section

ANTEBELLUM COURTSHIP INQUIRY

(He) Is you a flyin' lark or a settin' dove?
(She) I'se a flyin' lark, my honey Love.
(He) Is you a bird o' one fedder, or a bird o' two?
(She) I'se a bird o' one fedder, w'en it comes to you.
(He) Den, Mam:
I has desire, an' quick temptation,
To jine my fence to yō' plantation.

INVITED TO TAKE THE ESCORT'S ARM

Miss, does you lak strawberries?

____*____*____*____*____*____

Den hang on de vine.

____*____*____*____*____*____

Miss, does you lak chicken?

____*____*____*____*____*____

Den have a wing dis time.

SPARKING OR COURTING

I'se heaps older dan three.
I'se heaps thicker dan barks;
An' de older I gits,
De mō' harder I sparks.

I sparks fast an' hard,
For I'se feared I mought fail.
Dough I'se gittin' ole,
I don't co't lak no snail.

A CLANDESTINE LETTER

Kind Miss: If I sent you a letter,
By de crickets,
Through de thickets,
How'd you answer better?

Kind Suh: I'd sen' you a letter,
By de mole,
Not to be tōl';
Fer dat's mō' secretter.

ANTEBELLUM MARRIAGE PROPOSAL

(A proposal of marriage with the answer deferred)

(He) De ocean, it's wide; de sea, it's deep.
Yes, in yō' arms I begs to sleep,
Not fer one time, not fer three;
But long as we-uns can agree.

(She) Please gimme time, Suh, to "re-ponder;"
Please gimme time to "gargalize;"
Den 'haps I'll tu'n to "cattlegog,"
An' answer up 'greeable fer a s'prise.

IF YOU FROWN

If you frowns, an' I frowns,
W'en we goes out togedder;
Den all de t'other folks aroun'
Will say: "De rain is fallin' down
Right in de sunshine wedder!"

"LET'S MARRY" COURTSHIP

(A proposal of marriage, with a provisional acceptance)

(HE) Oh Miss Lizie, how I loves you!
My life's jes los' if you hain't true.
If you loves me lak I loves you,
No knife cain't cut our love in two.

(She) Grapevine warp, an' cornstalk fillin';
I'll marry you if mammy an' daddy's willin'.

(He) Rabbit hop an' long dog trot!
Let's git married if dey say "not."

COURTSHIP

(A proposal of marriage with its acceptance)

KIND MISS: I'se on de stage o' action,
Pleadin' hard fer satisfaction,
Pleadin' 'fore de time-thief late;
Darfore, Ma'm, now, *"cravenate."

* Cravenate = consider.

If I brung to you a gyarment;
To be cut widout scissors,
An' to be sewed widout thread;
How (I ax you) would you
make it,
Widout de needle sewin'
An' widout de cloth spread?

Kind Suh: I'd make dat gyarment
Wid love from my heart,
Wid tears on yō' head;
We never would part.

I WALKED THE ROADS

WELL: I walked de roads, till de roads git muddy.
I talked to dat pretty gal, till I couldn' stan' study.

Den: I say: "Love me liddle," I say; "Love me long."
I say: "Let dat liddle be 'doggone' strong!
For, shore as dat rat runs 'cross de rafter,
So shore you'se de gal, you'se de gal I'se after."

PRESENTING A HAT TO PHOEBE

SISTER PHOEBE: Happy wus we,
W'en we sot under dat Juniper tree.
Take dis hat, it'll keep yō' head warm.
Take dis kiss, it'll do you no harm.

Sister Phoebe: De hours, dey're few;
But dis hat'll say I'se thinkin' 'bout you.
Sugar, it's sugar; an' salt, it's salt;
If you don't love me, it's shō' yō' own fault.

WOOING

W'AT is dat a wukin
At yō' han' bill on de wall,
So's yō' sperit, it cain't res',
An' a gemmun's heat, it call?

Is you lookin' fer sweeter berries
Growin' on a higher bush?
An' does my combersation suit?
If not, w'at does you wush?

Courtship Song Rhyme Section

THE COURTING BOY

W'en I wus a liddle boy,
Jes fifteen inches high;
De way I court de pretty gals,
It make de ole folks cry.

De geese swim in de middle pon'.
De ducks fly 'cross de clover.
Run an' tell dem pretty gals,
Dat I'se a-comin' over.

Ho! Marindie! Ho!
Ho! Missindie! Ho!
Ho! Malindie! Ho! my gal!
I'se gwine now to see ole Sal.

PRETTY POLLY ANN

I'se gwineter marry, if I can.
I'se gwineter marry pretty Polly Ann.

I axed Polly Ann, fer to marry me.
She say she's a-lookin' fer a Nigger dat's
free.

Pretty Polly Ann's jes dressed so fine!
I'll bet five dollars she hain't got a dime.

Pretty Polly Ann's jes a-puttin' on airs,
She won't notice me, but nobody cares.

I'll drop Polly Ann, a-lookin' lak a crane;
I 'spec's I'll marry Miss Lize Jane.

Marriage Rhyme Section

SLAVE MARRIAGE CEREMONY SUPPLEMENT

Dark an' stormy may come de wedder;
I jines dis he-male an' dis she-male to-
gedder.
Let none, but Him dat makes de thunder,
Put dis he-male an' dis she-male asunder.
I darfore 'nounce you bofe de same.
Be good, go 'long, an' keep up yō' name.
De broomstick's jumped, de worl's not
wide.
She's now yō' own. Salute yō' bride!

Married Life Rhyme Section

THE NEWLY WEDS

First Mont': "Set down in my cabin, Honey!"
Nex' Mont': 'Stan' up, my Pie."
Third Mont': 'You go to wuk, you Wench!
You well to wuk as I!"

WHEN I GO TO MARRY

W'en I goes to marry,
I wants a gal wid money.
I wants a pretty black-eyed gal
To kiss an' call me "Honey."

Well, w'en I goes to marry,
I don't wanter git no riches.
I wants a man 'bout four
foot high,
So's I can w'ar de britches.

BOUGHT ME A WIFE

BOUGHT me a wife an' de wife please me,
I feeds my wife un'er yon'er tree.
My wife go: "Row-row!"
My guinea go: "Potrack! Potrack!
My chicken go: "Gymsack! Gymsack!"
My duck go: "Quack-quack! Quack-quack!"
My dog go: "Bow-bow!"
My hoss go: "Whee-whee! Whee-whee!"
My cat go: "Fiddle-toe! Fiddle-toe!"

WHEN I WAS A "ROUSTABOUT"

W'EN I wus a "Roustabout," wild an' young,
I co'ted my gal wid a mighty slick tongue.
I tōl' her some oncommon lies dere an' den.
I tōl' her dat we'd marry, but I didn' say w'en.

So on a Mond'y mornin' I tuck her fer my wife.
Of co'se I wus 'spectin' an agreeable life.
But on a Chuesd'y mornin' she chuned up her pipe,
An' she 'bused me more 'an I'd been 'bused all my life.

On a Wednesd'y evenin', as I come 'long home,
I says to myse'f dat she wus all my own;
An' on a Thursd'y night I went out to de woods,
An' I cut me two big fine tough leatherwoods.

So on a Frid'y mornin' w'en she roll me 'er eyes,
I retched fer my leatherwoods to give 'er a s'prise,
Dem long keen leatherwoods wuked mighty well,
An' 'er tongue, it jes rattle lak a clapper in a bell.

On a Sadd'y mornin' she sleep sorter late;
An' de las' time I see'd her, she 'us gwine out de gate.
I wus feedin' at de stable, lookin' out through a crack,
An' she lef' my log cabin 'fore I could git back.

On a Sund'y mornin', as I laid on my bed,
I didn' have no Nigger wife to bother my head.
Now whisky an' brandy jug's my biges' bes' friend,
An' my long week's wuk is about at its end.

MY FIRST AND MY SECOND WIFE

My fust liddle wife wus short an' fat.
Her face wus as black as my ole hat,
Her nose all flat, an' her eyes sunk in,
An' dat lip hang down below her chin.
Now wusn't I sorrowful in mind?

W'en I went down to dat wife's brother;
He said: "She 'us tired. Gwineter marry 'nother."
If I ever ketches dat city Coon,
He railly mought see my razzer soon.
Den I 'spec's he'd be troubled in mind!

My nex' wife hug an' kiss me,
She call me "Sugar Plum!"
She throw her arms 'round me,
Lak a grapevine 'round de gum!
Wusn't dat glory to my soul!

Her cheeks, dey're lak de cherry;
Dat Cherry, it's lak de rose.
Wid a liddle dimple in her chin,
An' a liddle tu'ned up nose!
Oh, hain't I happy in mind!

I'se got you, Lou, now fer my wife.
Keep new Coons 'way, "My Pie!"
Caze, if you don't, I tells you now,
Dat we all three mought die.
    Den we'd be troubled in min'!

GOOD-BY, WIFE!

I HAD a liddle wife,
An' I didn' want to kill 'er;
So I tuck 'er by de heels,
An' I throwed 'er in de river.
"Good-by, Wife! Good-by, Honey!
Hadn' been fer you,
I'd a had a liddle money."

My liddle fussy wife
Up an' say she mus' have scissors;
An' druther dan to fight,
I'd a throwed 'er in three rivers.
But she crossed dem fingers, w'en she go
    down,
An' a liddle bit later
She walk out on de groun'.

NURSERY RHYME SECTION

*AWFUL HARBINGERS

W'EN de big owl whoops,
An' de screech owl screeks,
An' de win' makes a howlin' sound;
You liddle wooly heads
Had better kiver up,
Caze de "hants" is comin' 'round.

THE LAST OF JACK

I HAD a liddle dog, his name wus Jack;
He run forty mile 'fore he look back.
W'en he look back, he fall in a crack;
W'en he fall in a crack, he break 'is back;
An' dat wus de las' o' poor liddle Jack.

*This little rhyme is based upon a superstition once current among Negroes, to the effect that bad luck would come when a screech owl called near your home at night unless, upon hearing him, you would stick the handle of a shovel into the fire about which you were sitting, or would throw salt into it. The word "hant" means ghost or spirit.

LITTLE DOGS

I HAD a liddle dog; his name wus Ball;
W'en I give him a liddle, he want it all.

I had a liddle dog, his name wus Trot;
He helt up his tail, all tied in a knot.

I had a liddle dog, his name wus Blue;
I put him on de road, an' he almos' flew.

I had a liddle dog, his name wus Mack;
I rid his tail fer to save his back.

I had a liddle dog, his name wus Rover;
W'en he died, he died all over.

I had a liddle dog, his name wus Dan;
An' w'en he died, I buried 'im in de san'.

MY DOG, CUFF

I HAD a liddle dog, his name wus Cuff;
I sent 'im to town to buy some snuff.
He drapped de bale, an' he spilt de snuff,
An' I guess dat speech is long enough.

SAM IS A CLEVER FELLOW

SAY! Is yō' peaches ripe, my boy,
An' is yō' apples meller?
Go an' tell Miss Katie Jones
Dat Sam's a clever feller.

Say! Is yō' cherries red, my boy,
An' is yō' plums all yeller?
Oh please run tell Miss Katie Jones
Dat Sam's a clever feller.

THE GREAT OWL'S SONG

AH-HOO-HOO? Ah-hoo-hoo? Ah-hoo-hoo——?
An' who'll cook fer Kelline, an' who'll cook fer you——?
I will cook fer myse'f, I won't cook fer you.
Ah-hoo-hoo! Ah-hoo-hoo! Ah-hoo——!

Ah-hoo-hoo! Ah-hoo-hoo! Ah-hoo-hoo! Ah-hoo——!
I wonder if Kelline would not cook fer Hue——?
Fer dis is Big Sandy! It's Big Sandy Hue——!
Ah-hoo-hoo! Ah-hoo-hoo! Ah-hoo-hoo! Ah-hoo——!

Ah-ha-hah! Ah-ha-hah! Ah-ha-hah! Ah-hah——!
I thought you 'us ole Bill Jack as black as de tah.
You really must 'scuse me, my "Honey Lump Pa."
Ah-ha-hah! Ah-ha-hah! Ah-ha-hah! Ah-hah——!

An' since I'se been Kelline, an' you'se Big Sandy Hue;
I will cook fer myse'f, an' I will cook fer you.
I'll love you forever, an' sing in de dew:
"Ah-hoo-hoo! Ah-hoo-hoo! Ah-hoo-hoo! Ah-hoo——!"

Yes!—Ah-hoo-hoo! Ah-hoo-hoo! Ah-hoo-hoo! Ah-hoo-all!
Now, we'll cook fer ourse'fs, but who'll cook fer you all?
Fer Tom Dick an' his wife, fer Pete Snap an' Shoe-Awl,
Rough Shot De Shoe-boot, an' de Lawd He knows who all?

HERE I STAND

HERE I stan', raggity an' dirty;
If you don't come kiss me, I'll run lak a
    tucky.

Here I stan' on two liddle chips,
Pray, come kiss my sweet liddle lips.

Here I stan' crooked lak a horn;
I hain't had no kiss since I'se been born.

PIG TAIL

RUN boys, run!
De pig tail's done.
If you don't come quick,
You won't git none.

Pig ham's dere,
Lakwise middlin's square;
But dese great big parts
Hain't no Nigger's bes' fare.

A, B, C

A, B, C,
Doubled down D;
I'se so lazy you cain't see me.

A, B, C,
Doubled down D
Lazy Chilluns gits hick'ry tea.

A, B, C,
Doubled down D,
Dat "cat's" in de cupboard an' hid. You see?

A, B, C,
Doubled down D,
You'd better come out an' wuk lak me.

NEGRO BAKER MAN

PATTY cake! Patty cake! Nigger Baker man.
Missus an' Mosser gwineter ketch 'im if dey can.
Put de liddle Nigger in Mosser's dish pan,
An' scrub 'im off good fer de ole San' Man.

STICK-A-MA-STEW

STICK-A-MA-STEW, he went to town.
Stick-a-ma-stew, he tore 'is gown.
All dem folks what live in town
Cain't mend dat randsome, handsome
gown.

BOB-WHITE'S SONG

BOB-WHITE! Bob-white!
Is yō' peas all ripe?
No—! not—! quite!

Bob-white! Bob-white!
W'en will dey be ripe?
To-mor—! row—! might!

Bob-white! Bob-white!
Does you sing at night?
No—! not—! quite!

Bob-white! Bob-white!
W'en is de time right?
At can—! dle—! light!

COOKING DINNER

Go: BILE dem cabbage down.
Turn dat hoecake 'round,
Cook it done an' brown.

Yes: Gwineter have sweet taters too.
Hain't had none since las' Fall,
Gwineter eat 'em skins an' all.

CHUCK WILL'S WIDOW SONG

OH nimber, nimber Will-o!
My crooked, crooked bill-o!
I'se settin' down right now, on
de sweet pertater hill-o.

Oh nimber, nimber Will-o!
My crooked, crooked bill-o!
Two liddle naked babies, my two
brown aigs now fill-o.

Oh nimber, nimber Will-o!
My crooked, crooked bill-o!
Don't hurt de liddle babies; dey
is too sweet to kill-o.

BRIDLE UP A RAT

BRIDLE up er rat,
Saddle up er cat,
An' han' me down my big straw hat.

In come de cat,
Out go de rat,
Down go de baby wid 'is big straw hat.

MY LITTLE PIG

YOU SEE: I had a liddle pig,
I fed 'im on slop;
He got so fat
Dat he almos' pop.

An' den: I tuck de liddle pig,
An' I rid 'im to school;
He e't ginger cake,
An' it tu'n 'im a fool.

But he grunt de lessons,
An' keep all de rule,
An' he make 'em all think
Dat he learn in de cool.

IN A MULBERRY TREE

JES looky, looky yonder; w'at I see!
Two liddle Niggers in a Mulberry tree.
One cain't read, an' de t'other cain't write.
But dey bofe can smoke deir daddy's pipe.

"One ma two! One ma two!"
Dat Mulberry Witch, he *titterer too.
"Big bait o' Mulberries make 'em bofe sick.
Dem liddle Niggers gwineter roll an' kick!"

ANIMAL ATTIRE

DAT Coon, he w'ar a undershirt;
Dat 'Possum w'ar a gown.
Br'er Rabbit, he w'ar a overcoat
Wid buttons up an' down.

Mistah Gobbler's got beads 'roun' 'is nec'.
Mistah Pattridge's got a collar, Hun!
Mistah Peacock, a fedder on his head!
But dese don't stop no gun.

* Titterer means laugh.

ASPIRATION

If I wus de President
Of dese United States,
I'd eat good 'lasses candy,
An' swing on all de gates.

ANIMAL FAIR

Has you ever hearn tell 'bout de Animal Fair?
Dem birds an' beasts wus all down dere.
Dat jaybird a-settin' down on 'is wing!
Has you ever hearn tell about sitch a thing
As whut 'us at dat Animal Fair?

Well, dem animals had a Fair.
Dem birds an' beasts wus dere.
De big Baboon,
By de light o' de moon,
Jes comb up his sandy hair.

De monkey, he git drunk,
He kick up a red hot chunk.
Dem coals, dey 'rose;
An' bu'nt 'is toes!
He clumb de Elephan's trunk.

I went down to de Fair.
Dem varmints all wus dere.
Dat young Baboon
Wunk at Miss Coon;
Dat curled de Elephan's hair.

De Camel den walk 'bout,
An' tromped on de Elephan's
snout.
De Elephan' sneeze,
An' fall on his knees;
Dat pleased all dem monkēys.

LITTLE BOY WHO COULDN'T COUNT SEVEN

ONCE der wus a liddle boy dat couldn' count one.
Dey pitched him in a fedder bed; 'e thought it
great big fun.

Once der wus a liddle boy dat couldn' count two.
Dey pitched him in a fedder bed; 'e thought 'e 'us
gwine through.

Once der wus a liddle boy dat couldn' count three.
Dey pitched him in a fedder bed; 'e thought de
Niggers 'us free.

Once der wus a liddle boy dat couldn' count fō'.
Dey pitched him in a fedder bed; 'e jumped out
on de flō'.

Once der wus a liddle boy dat couldn' count five.
Dey pitched him in a fedder bed; 'e thought de
dead alive.

Once der wus a liddle boy dat couldn' count six.
Dey pitched him in a fedder bed; 'e never did git
fix!

Once der wus a liddle boy dat couldn' count seben.
Dey pitched him in a fedder bed; 'e thought he's
gwine to Heaben!

MISS TERRAPIN AND MISS TOAD

As I went marchin' down de road,
I met Miss Tearpin an' I met Miss Toad.
An' ev'ry time Miss Toad would jump,
Miss Tearpin would peep from 'hind de stump.

I axed dem ladies fer to marry me,
An' bofe find fault wid de t'other, you see.
"If you marries Miss Toad," Miss Tearpin said,
"You'll have to hop 'round lak you'se been half dead!"

"If you combs yō' head wid a Tearpin comb,
You'll have to creep 'round all tied up at home."
I run'd away frum dar, my foot got bruise,
For I didn't know zackly which to choose.

FROM SLAVERY

CHILE: I come from out'n slavery,
Whar de Bull-whup bust de hide;
Back dar, whar dis gineration
Natchully widdered up an' died!

THE END OF TEN LITTLE NEGROES

TEN liddle Niggers, a-eatin', fat an' fine;
One choke hisse'f to death, an' dat lef' nine.
Nine liddle Niggers, dey sot up too late;
One sleep hisse'f to death, an' dat lef' eight.
Eight liddle Niggers want to go to Heaben;
One sing hisse'f to death, an' dat lef' seben.
Seben liddle Niggers, a-pickin' up sticks;
One wuk hisse'f to death, an' dat lef' six.
Six liddle Niggers went out fer to drive;
Mule run away wid one, an' dat lef' five.
Five liddle Niggers in a cold rain pour;
One coughed hisse'f to death, an' dat lef' four.
Four liddle Niggers, climb a' apple tree;
One fall down an' out, an' dat lef' three.
Three liddle Niggers a-wantin' sumpin new;
One, he quit de udders, an' dat lef' two.
Two liddle Niggers went out fer to run;
One fell down de bluff, an' dat lef' one.
One liddle Nigger, a-foolin' wid a gun;
Gun go off "bang!" an' dat lef' none.

THE ALABAMA WAY

'Way down yon'er "in de Alerbamer way,"
De Niggers goes to wo'k at de peep o' de day.
De bed's too short, an' de high posts rear;
De Niggers needs a ladder fer to climb up dere.
De cord's wore out, an' de bed-tick's gone.
Niggers' legs hang down fer de chickens t' roost on.

MOTHER SAYS I AM SIX YEARS OLD

My mammy says dat I'se too young
To go to Church an' pray;
But she don't know how bad I is
W'en she's been gone away.

My mammy says I'se six years old,
My daddy says I'se seben.
Dat's all right how old I is,
Jes since I'se a gwine to Heaben.

THE ORIGIN OF THE SNAKE

Up de hill an' down de level!
Up de hill an' down de level!
Granny's puppy treed de Devil.

Puppy howl, an' Devil shake!
Puppy howl, an' Devil shake!
Devil leave, an' dere's yō' snake.

Mash his head; dc sun shine bright!
Mash his head; de sun shine bright;
Tail don't die ontel it's night.

Night come on, an' sperits groan!
Night come on, an' sperits groan!
Devil come an' gits his own.

WILD HOG HUNT

Nigger in de woods, a-settin' on a log;
Wid his finger on de trigger, an' his eyes
upon de hog.
De gun say "bam!" an' de hog say "bip!"
An' de Nigger grab dat wild hog wid all
his grip.

A STRANGE BROOD

DE ole hen sot on tucky aigs,
An' she hatch out goslin's three.
Two wus tuckies wid slender legs,
An' one wus a bumblebee.
All dem hens say to one nudder:
"Mighty queer chickens! See?"

THE TOWN AND THE COUNTRY BIRD

JAYBIRD a-swingin' a two hoss plow;
"Sparrer, why not you?"
"W'y—! My legs so liddle an' slen-
der, man,
I'se fear'd dey'd break in two."

Jaybird answer: "What'd you say?—
I sometimes worms terbaccy;
But I'd druther plow sweet taters too,
Dan to be a ole Town Tacky!"

Jaybird up in de Sugar tree,
De sparrer on de groun';
De jaybird shake de sugar down,
An' de sparrer pass it 'roun'.

De jaybird say: "Save some fer me;
I needs it w'en I bakes."
De sparrer say: "Use 'lasses, Suh!
Dat suits fer Country-Jakes!"

FROG IN A MILL (* GUINEA OR EBO RHYME)

Once dere wus er frog dat lived in er mill.
He had er raker don la bottom o' la kimebo
Kimebo, nayro, dilldo, kiro
Stimstam, formididdle, all-a-board la rake;
Wid er raker don la bottom o' la kimebo.

STRONG HANDS

Here's yō' bread, an' here's yō' butter;
An' here's de hands fer to make you sputter.

Tetch dese hands, w'en you wants to tetch a beaver.
If dese hands tetch you, you'll shō' ketch de fever.

Dese hands Samson, good fer a row,
W'en dey hits you, it's "good-by cow!"

* For explanation, read the Study in Negro Folk Rhymes.

TREE FROGS (GUINEA OR EBO RHYME)

Shool! Shool! Shool!
I rule!
Shool! Shool! Shool! I
rule!
Shool! Shacker-rack!
I shool bubba cool.

Seller! Beller eel!
Fust to ma tree'l
Just came er bubba.
Buska! Buska-reel!

WHEN I WAS A LITTLE BOY

W'en I wus a liddle boy
I cleaned up mammy's dishes;
Now I is a great big boy,
I wears my daddy's britches.
I can knock dat Mobile Buck
An' smoke dat corncob pipe.
I can kiss dem pretty gals,
An' set up ev'ry night.

GRASSHOPPER SENSE

DERE wus a liddle grasshopper
Dat wus always on de jump;
An' caze he never look ahead,
He wus always gittin' a bump.

Huddlety, dumpty, dumpty, dump!
Mind out, or you will git a bump;
Shore as de grass grows 'round de stump
Be keerful, my sweet Sugar Lump.

YOUNG MASTER AND OLD MASTER

HICK'RY leaves an' calico sleeves!
I tells you young Mosser's hard to please.
Young Mosser fool you, de way he grin.
De way he whup you is a sin.

De monkey's a-settin' on de end of a rail,
Pickin' his tooth wid de end of his tail.
Mulberry leaves an' homespun sleeves!
Better know dat ole Mosser's not easy to
please.

MY SPECKLED HEN

Somebody stole my speckled hen.
Dey lef' me mighty pōo'.
Ev'ry day she layed three aigs,
An' Sunday she lay fō'.

Somebody stole my speckled hen.
She crowed at my back dō'.
Fedders, dey shine jes lak de sun;
De Niggers grudged her mō'.

* De whis'lin' gal, an' de crowin' hen,
Never comes to no good en'.
Stop dat whis'lin'; go on an' sing!
'Member dat hen wid 'er shinin' wing.

THE SNAIL'S REPLY

Snail! Snail! Come out'n o' yō' shell,
Or I'll beat on yō' back till you rings lak a bell.

"I do ve'y well," sayed de snail in de shell,
"I'll jes take my chances in here whar I dwell."

* An old superstition.

A STRANGE FAMILY

ONCE dere's an ole 'oman dat lived
in de Wes'.
She had two gals of de very bes'.
One wus older dan de t'other,
T'other's older dan her mother,
An' dey're all deir own gran'mother.
Can you guess?

GOOD-BY, RING

I HAD a liddle dog, his name wus Ring,
I tied him up to his nose wid a string.
I pulled dat string, an' his eyes tu'n blue.
"Good-by, Ring! I'se done wid you."

DEEDLE, DUMPLING

DEEDLE, deedle, dumplin'! My boy, Pete!
He went to bed wid his dirty feet.
Mammy laid a switch down on dat sheet!
Deedle, deedle, dumplin'! My boy, Pete!

BUCK AND BERRY

BUCK an' Berry run a race,
Buck fall down an' skin his face.

Buck an' Berry in a stall;
Buck, he try to eat it all.

Buck, he e't too much, you see.
So he died wid choleree.

PRETTY LITTLE GIRL

WHO's been here since I'se been gone?
A pretty liddle gal wid a blue dress on.

Who'll stay here when I goes 'way?
A pretty liddle gal, all dressed in gray.

Who'll wait on Mistess day an' night?
A pretty liddle gal, all dressed in white.

Who'll be here when I'se been dead?
A pretty liddle gal, all dressed in red.

TWO SICK NEGRO BOYS

Two liddle Niggers sick in bed,
One jumped up an' bumped his head.
W'en de Doctah come he simpully said:
"Jes feed dat boy on shorten' bread."

T'other liddle Nigger sick in bed,
W'en he hear tell o' shorten' bread,
Popped up all well. He dance an'
sing!
He almos' cut dat Pigeon's Wing!

GRASSHOPPER SITTING ON A SWEET POTATO VINE

GRASSHOPPER a settin' on a sweet tater vine,
'Long come a Blackbird an' nab him up behind.

Blackbird a-settin' in a sour apple tree;
Hawk grab him up behind; he "Chee! Chee!
Chee!"

Big hawk a-settin' in de top of dat oak,
Start to eat dat Blackbird an' he git choke.

DOODLE-BUG

DOODLE-BUG! Doodle-bug! Come git sweet milk.
Doodle-bug! Doodle-bug! Come git butter.
Doodle bug! Doodle-bug! Come git co'n bread.
Doodle-bug! Doodle-bug! Come on to Supper.

* RAW HEAD AND BLOODY BONES

DON'T talk! Go to sleep!
Eyes shet an' don't you peep!
Keep still, or he jes moans:
"Raw Head an' Bloody Bones!"

MYSTERIOUS FACE WASHING

I WASH my face in de watah
Dat's neider rain nor run.
I wipes my face on de towel
Dat's neider wove nor spun.—
I wash my face in de dew,
An' I dries it in de sun.

* Repeated to restless children at night to make them lie still and go to sleep.

GO TO BED

De wood's in de kitchen.
De hoss's in de shed.
You liddle Niggers
Had better go to bed.

* BUCK-EYED RABBIT! WHOOPEE!

Dat Squir'l, he's a cunnin' thing;
He tote a bushy tail.
He jes lug off Uncle Sambo's co'n,
An' heart it on a rail.

Dat Squir'l, he's a cunnin' thing;
An' so is ole Jedge B'ar.
Br'er Rabbit's gone an' los' his tail
'Cep' a liddle bunch of ha'r.

Buckeyed Rabbit! Whoopee!
Buckeyed Rabbit! Ho!
Buckeyed Rabbit! Whoopee!
Squir'l's got a long way to go.

* The explanation of this rhyme is found in the Study in Negro Folk Rhymes.

CAPTAIN COON

CAPTAIN COON's a mighty man,
He trabble atter dark;
Wid nothin' 'tall to 'sturb his mind,
But to hear my ole dog bark.

Dat 'Possum, he's a mighty man,
He trabble late at night.
He never think to climb a tree,
'Till he's feared ole Rober'll bite.

GUINEA GALL

'WAY down yon'er in Guinea Gall,
De Niggers eats de fat an' all.
'Way down yon'er in de cotton fiel',
Ev'ry week one peck o' meal.
'Way down yon'er ole Mosser swar';
Holler at you, an' pitch, an' r'ar;
    Wid cat o' nine tails,
    Wid pen o' nine nails,
    Tee whing, tee bing,
    An' ev'ry thing!

FISHING SIMON

SIMON tuck his hook an' pole,
An' fished on Sunday we's been told.
Fish dem water death bells ring,
Talk from out'n de water, sing—
"Bait yō' hook, Simon!
Drap yō' line, Simon!
Now ketch me, Simon!
Pull me out, Simon!
Take me home, Simon!
Now clean me, Simon!
Cut me up now, Simon!
Now salt me, Simon!
Now fry me, Simon!
Dish me up now, Simon!
Eat me all, Simon!"
Simon e't till he wus full.
Still dat fish keep his plate fall.
Simon want no mō' at all,
Fish say dat he mus' eat all.
Simon's sick, so he throw up!
He give Sunday fishin' up.

A STRANGE OLD WOMAN

Dere wus an ole 'oman, her name wus Nan.
She lived an 'oman, an' died a man.
De ole 'oman lived to be dried up an' cunnin';
One leg stood still, while de tother kep' runnin'.

IN '76

Way down yonder in sebenty-six,
Whar I git my jawbone fix;
All dem coon-loons eatin' wid a spoon!
I'll be ready fer dat Great Day soon.

REDHEAD WOODPECKER

Redhead woodpecker: "Chip! Chip! Chee!"
Promise dat he'll marry me.
Whar shall de weddin' supper be?
Down in de lot, in a rotten holler tree.
What will de weddin' supper be?
A liddle green worm an' a bumblebee,
'Way down yonder on de holler tree.
De Redhead woodpecker, "Chip! Chip! Chee!"

OLD AUNT KATE

JES look at Ole Aunt Kate at de gyardin gate!
She's a good ole 'oman.
W'en she sift 'er meal, she give me de husk;
W'en she cook 'er bread, she give me de crust.
She put de hosses in de stable;
But one jump out, an' skin his nable.
Jes look at Ole Aunt Kate at de gyardin gate!
Still she's always late.

Hurrah fer Ole Aunt Kate by de gyardin gate!
She's a fine ole 'oman.
Git down dat sifter, take down dat tray!
Go 'long, Honey, dere hain't no udder way!
She put on dat hoe cake, she went 'round de house.
She cook dat 'Possum, an' she call 'im a mouse!
Hurrah fer Ole Aunt Kate by de gyardin gate!
She's a fine playmate.

CHILDREN'S SEATING RHYME

YOU set outside, an' ketch de cow-hide.
I'll set in de middle, an' play de gol' fiddle.
You set 'round about, an' git scrouged out.

MY BABY

I'se de daddy of dis liddle black baby.
He's his mammy's onliest sweetest liddle Coon.
Got de look on de forehead lak his daddy,
Pretty eyes jes as big as de moon.

I'se de daddy of dis liddle black baby.
Yes, his mammy keep de "Sugar" rollin' over.
She feed him wid a tin cup an' a spoon;
An' he kick lak a pony eatin' clover.

A RACE-STARTER'S RHYME

One fer de money!
Two fer de show!
Three to git ready,
An' four fer to go!

NESTING

De jaybird build on a swingin' lim',
De sparrow in de gyardin;
Dat ole gray goose in de panel o' de fence,
An' de gander on de t'other side o' Jordan.

BABY WANTS CHERRIES

De cherries, dey're red; de cherries, dey're ripe;
An' de baby it want one.
De cherries, dey're hard; de cherries, dey're sour;
An' de baby cain't git none.

Jes look at dat bird in de cherry tree!
He's pickin' 'em one by one!
He's shakin' his bill, he's gittin' it fill',
An' down dat th'oat dey run!

Nev' mind! Bye an' bye dat bird's gwineter fly,
An' mammy's gwineter make dat pie.
She'll give you a few, fer de baby cain't chew,
An' de Pickaninny sholy won't cry.

A PRETTY PAIR OF CHICKENS

Dat box-legged rooster, an' dat bow-legged hen
Make a mighty pretty couple, not to be no kin.
Dey's jes lak some Niggers wearin' white folks ole britches,
Dey thinks dey's lookin' fine, w'en dey needs lots of stitches.

TOO MUCH WATERMELON

Dere wus a great big watermillion growin' on de vine.
Dere wus a liddle ugly Nigger watchin' all de time.
An' w'en dat great big watermillion lay ripenin' in de sun,
An' de stripes along its purty skin wus comin' one by one,
Dat ugly Nigger pulled it off an' toted it away,
An' he e't dat great big watermillion all in one single day.
He e't de rinds, an' red meat too, he finish it all trim;
An' den,—dat great big watermillion up an' finish him.

BUTTERFLY

Pretty liddle butterfly, yaller as de gold,
My sweet liddle butterfly, you shō' is mighty bold.
You can dance out in de sun, you can fly up high,
But you know I'se bound to git you, yet, my liddle butterfly.

THE HATED BLACKBIRD AND CROW

DAT Blackbird say unto de Crow:
"Dat's why de white folks hates us so;
For ever since ole Adam wus born,
It's been our rule to gedder green corn."

Dat Blackbird say unto de Crow:
"If you's not black, den I don't know.
White folks calls you black, but I say not;
Caze de kittle musn' talk about de pot."

IN A RUSH

HERE I comes jes a-rearin' an' a-pitchin',
I hain't had no kiss since I lef' de ole kitchin.
Candy, dat's sweet; dat's very, very clear;
But a kiss from yō' lips would be sweeter, my dear.

TAKING A WALK

WE's a-walkin' in de green grass dust, dust, dust.
We's a-walkin' in de green grass dust.
If you's jes as sweet as I thinks you to be,
I'll take you by yō' liddle hand to walk wid me.

PAYING DEBTS WITH KICKS

I owes yō' daddy a peck o' peas.
I'se gwineter pay it wid my knees.
I owes yō' mammy a pound o' meat;
An' I'se gwineter pay dat wid my feet.
Now, if I owes 'em somethin' mō';
You come right back an' let me know.
Please say to dem ('fore I fergets)
I never fails to pay my debts.

GETTING TEN NEGRO BOYS TOGETHER

One liddle Nigger boy whistle an' stew,
He whistle up anudder Nigger an' dat make two.
Two liddle Nigger boys shuck de apple tree,
Down fall anudder Nigger, an' dat make three.
Three liddle Nigger boys, a-wantin' one more,
Never has no trouble a-gittin' up four.
Four liddle Nigger boys, dey cain't drive.
Dey hire a Nigger hack boy, an' dat make five.
Five liddle Niggers, bein' calcullated men,
Call anudder Nigger 'piece an' dat make ten.

HAWK AND CHICKENS

Hen an' chickens in a fodder stack,
Mighty busy scratchin'.
Hawk settin' off on a swingin' lim',
Ready fer de catchin'.

Hawk come a-whizzin' wid his bitin' mouf,
Couldn' hold hisself in.
Hen, flyin' up, knock his eye clean out;
An' de Jaybird died a-laughin'.

MUD-LOG POND

As I stepped down by de Mud-log pon',
I seed dat bullfrog wid his shoe-boots on.
His eyes wus glass, an' his heels wus brass;
An' I give him a dollar fer to let me pass.

WHAT WILL WE DO FOR BACON?

What will we do fer bacon now?
I'se shot, I'se shot de ole sandy sow!
She jumped de fence an' broke de rail;
An'—"Bam!"—I shot her on de tail.

A LITTLE PICKANINNY

ME an' its mammy is both gwine to town,
To git dis Pickaninny a liddle hat an' gown.
Don't you never let him waller on de flō'!
He's a liddle Pickaninny,
Born in ole Virginy.
Mammy! Don't de baby grow?

Setch a eatin' o' de honey an' a drinkin' o' de wine!
We's gwine down togedder fer to have a good time;
An' we's gwineter eat, an' drink mō' an' mō'.
Oh, sweet liddle * Pickaninny,
Born in ole Virginy.
Mammy! How de baby grow!

† DON'T SING BEFORE BREAKFAST

DON'T sing out 'fore Breakfast,
Don't sing 'fore you eat,
Or you'll cry out 'fore midnight,
You'll cry 'fore you sleep.

* Pickanniny appears to have been an African word used by the early American slaves for the word baby.
† A superstition.

MY FOLKS AND YOUR FOLKS

If you an' yō' folks
Likes me an' my folks,
Lak me an' my folks,
Likes you an' yō' folks;
You's never seed folks,
Since folks 'as been folks,
Like you an' yō' folks,
Lak me an' my folks.

LITTLE SLEEPING NEGROES

One liddle Nigger a-lyin' in de bed;
His eyes shet an' still, lak he been dead.

Two liddle Niggers a-lyin' in de bed;
A-snorin' an' a-dreamin' of a table spread.

Three liddle Niggers a-lyin' in de bed;
Deir heels cracked open lak shorten' bread.

Four liddle Niggers a-lyin' in de bed;
Dey'd better hop out, if dey wants to git fed!

MAMMA'S DARLING

WID flowers on my shoulders,
An' wid slippers on my feet;
I'se my mammy's darlin'.
Don't you think I'se sweet?

I wish I had a fourpence,
Den I mought use a dime.
I wish I had a Sweetheart,
To kiss me all de time.

I has apples on de table,
An' I has peaches on de shelf;
But I wish I had a husband—
I'se so tired stayin' to myself.

STEALING A RIDE

Two liddle Nigger boys as black as tar,
Tryin' to go to Heaben on a railroad chyar.
Off fall Nigger boys on a cross-tie!
Dey's gwineter git to Heaben shore bye-an'-bye.

WASHING MAMMA'S DISHES

WHEN I wus a liddle boy
A-washin' my mammy's dishes,
I rund my finger down my th'oat
An' pulled out two big fishes!

When I wus a liddle boy
A-wipin' my mammy's dishes,
I sticked my finger in my eye
An' I shō' seed liddle fishes.

De big fish swallowed dem all up!
It put me jes a-thinkin'.
All dem things looks awful cu'ous!
I wonder wus I drinkin'?

WILLIE WEE

WILLIE, Willie, Willie Wee!
One, two, three.
If you wanna kiss a pretty gal,
Come kiss me.

ONE NEGRO THEME SUNG WITH "FROG WENT A-COURTING"

FROG WENT A-COURTING

De frog went a-co'tin', he did ride. Uh-huh! Uh-
huh!
De frog went a-co'tin', he did ride
Wid a sword an' a pistol by 'is side. Uh-huhl
Uh-huh!

He rid up to Miss Mousie's dō'. Uh-huh! Uh-huh!
He rid up to Miss Mousie's dō',
Whar he'd of'en been befō. Uh-huh! Uh-huh!

Says he: "Miss Mousie, is you in?" Uh-huh! Uh-huh!
Says he: "Miss Mousie, is you in?"
"Oh yes, Sugar Lump! I kyard an' spin." Uh-huh! Uh-huh!

He tuck dat Mousie on his knee. Uh-huh! Uh-huh!
He tuck dat Mousie on his knee,
An' he say: "Dear Honey, marry me!" Uh-huh! Uh-huh!

"Oh Suh!" she say, 'I cain't do dat." Uh-huh! Uh-huh!
"Oh Suh!" she say, "I cain't do dat,
Widout de sayso o' uncle Rat." Uh-huh! Uh-huh!

Dat ole gray Rat, he soon come home. Uh-huh! Uh-huh!
Dat ole gray Rat, he soon come home,
Sayin': "Whose been here since I'se been gone?" Uh-huh! Uh-huh!

"A fine young gemmun fer to see." Uh-huh! Uh-huh!
"A fine young gemmun fer to see,
An' one dat axed fer to marry me." Uh-huh! Uh-huh!

Dat Rat jes laugh to split his side. Uh-huh!
Uh-huh!
Dat Rat jes laugh to split his side.
"Jes think o' Mousie's bein' a bride!" Uh-huh!
Uh-huh!

Nex' day, dat rat went down to town. Uh-huh!
Uh-huh!
Nex' day dat rat went down to town,
To git up de Mousie's Weddin' gown. Uh-huh!
Uh-huh!

"What's de bes' thing fer de Weddin' gown?"
Uh-huh! Uh-huh!
"What's de bes' thing fer de Weddin' gown?"—
"Dat acorn hull, all gray an' brown!" Uh-huh!
Uh-huh!

"Whar shall de Weddin' Infar' be?" Uh-huh!
Uh-huh!
"Whar shall de Weddin' Infar' be?"—
"Down in de swamp in a holler tree." Uh-huh!
Uh-huh!

"What shall de Weddin' Infar' be?" Uh-huh!
Uh-huh!
"What shall de Weddin' Infar' be?"—
"Two brown beans an' a blackeyed pea." Uh-huh!
Uh-huh!

Fust to come in wus de Bumblebee. Uh-huh!
Uh-huh!
Fust to come in wus de Bumblebee.
Wid a fiddle an' bow across his knee. Uh-huh!
Uh-huh!

De nex' dat come wus Khyernel Wren. Uh-huh!
Uh-huh!
De nex' dat come wus Khyernel Wren,
An' he dance a reel wid de Turkey Hen. Uh-huh!
Uh-huh!

De nex' dat come wus Mistah Snake. Uh-huh!
Uh-huh!
De nex' dat come wus Mistah Snake,
He swallowed de whole weddin' cake! Uh-huh!
Uh-huh!

De nex' come in wus Cap'n Flea. Uh-huh! Uh-huh!
De nex' come in wus Cap'n Flea,
An' he dance a jig fer de Bumblebee. Uh-huh! Uh-huh!

An' now come in ole Giner'l Louse. Uh-huh! Uh-huh!
An' now come in ole Giner'l Louse.
He dance a breakdown 'round de house. Uh-huh! Uh-huh!

De nex' to come wus Major Tick. Uh-huh! Uh-huh!
De nex' to come wus Major Tick,
An' he e't so much it make 'im sick. Uh-huh! Uh-huh!

Dey sent fer Mistah Doctah Fly. Uh-huh! Uh-huh!
Dey sent fer Mistah Doctah Fly.
Says he: "Major Tick, you's boun' to die." Uh-huh! Uh-huh!

Oh, den crep' in ole Mistah Cat. Uh-huh! Uh-huh!
Oh, den crep' in ole Mistah Cat,
An' chilluns, dey all hollered, "Scat!!" Uh-huh!!! Uh-huh!!!

It give dat frog a turble fright. Uh-huh! Uh-huh!
It give dat frog a turble fright,
An' he up an' say to dem, "Good-night!" Uh-huh! Uh-huh!

Dat frog, he swum de lake aroun'. Uh-huh! Uh-huh!
Dat frog, he swum de lake aroun',
An' a big black duck come gobble 'im down. Uh-huh! Uh-huh!

"What d'you say 'us Miss Mousie's lot?" Uh-huh! Uh-huh!
"What d'you say 'us Miss Mousie's lot?"—
"W'y—, she got swallered on de spot!" Uh-huh! Uh-huh!

Now, I don't know no mō' 'an dat. Uh-huh! Uh-huh!
Now, I don't know no mō' 'an dat.
If you gits mō' you can take my hat. Uh-huh! Uh-huh!

An' if you thinks dat hat won't do. Uh-huh! Uh-huh!
An' if you thinks dat hat won't do,
Den you mought take my head 'long, too. Uh-huh!!! Uh-huh!!!

SHOO! SHOO!

Shoo! Shoo!
What'll I do?
Run three mile an' buckle my shoe?

No! No!
I'se gwineter go,
An' kill dat chicken on my flō'.

Oh! My!
Chicken pie!
Sen' fer de Doctah, I mought die.

Christmus here,
Once a year.
Pass dat cider an' 'simmon beer.

FLAP-JACKS

I loves my wife, an' I loves my baby:
An' I loves dem flap-jacks a-floatin' in gravy.
You play dem chyards, an' make two passes:
While I eats dem flap-jacks a-floatin' in 'lasses.

Now: in come a Nigger an' in come a bear,
In come a Nigger dat hain't got no hair.
Good-by, Nigger, go right on back,
Fer I hain't gwineter give you no flap-jack.

TEACHING TABLE MANNERS

Now whilst we's here 'round de table,
All you young ones git right still.
I wants to l'arn you some good manners,
So's you'll think o' Uncle Bill.

Cose we's gwineter 'scuse Merlindy,
Caze she's jes a baby yit.
But it's time you udder young ones
Wus a-l'arnin' a liddle bit.

I can 'member as a youngster,
Lak you youngsters is to-day;
How my mammy l'arnt me manners
In a 'culiar kind o' way.

One o' mammy's ole time 'quaintance.
(Ole Aunt Donie wus her name)
Come one night to see my mammy.
Mammy co'se 'pared fer de same.

Mammy got de sifter, Honey;
An' she tuck an' make up dough,
Which she tụ'n into hot biscuits.
Den we all git smart, you know.

'Zerves an' biscuits on de table!
Honey, noways could I wait.
Ole Aunt Donie wus a good ole 'oman,
An' I jes had to pass my plate.

I soon swallered down dem biscuit,
E't 'em faster dan a shoat.
Dey wus a liddle tough an' knotty,
But I chawed 'em lak a goat.

"Pass de biscuits, please, Mam!
Please, Mam, fer I wants some mō'."
Lawd! You'd oughter seed my mammy
Frownin' up, jes "sorter so."

"Won't you pass de biscuit, please, Mam?"
I said wid a liddle fear.
Dere wus not but one mō' lef', Sir.
Mammy riz up out'n her chear.

W'en Aunt Donie lef' our house, Suh,
Mammy come lak bees an' ants,
Put my head down 'twixt her knees, Suh,
Almos' roll me out'n my pants.

She had a great big tough hick'ry,
An' it help till it convince.
Frum dat day clean down to dis one,
I'se had manners ev'r since.

MISS BLODGER

De rats an' de mice, dey rund up stairs,
Fer to hear Miss Blodger say her prayers.
Now here I stan's 'fore Miss Blodger.
She 'spects to hit me, but I'se gwineter dodge her.

THE LITTLE NEGRO FLY

Dere's a liddle Nigger fly
Got a pretty liddle eye;
But he don't know 'is A, B, C's.
He up an' crawl de book,
An' he eben 'pears to look;
But he don't know 'is A, B, C's.

DESTINIES OF GOOD AND BAD CHILDREN

ONE, two, three, fō', five, six, seben;
All de good chilluns goes to Heaben.
All de bad chilluns goes below,
To * segashuate wid ole man † Joe.

One, two, three, fō', five, six, seben, eight;
All de good chilluns goes in de Pearly Gate.
But all de bad chilluns goes the Broad Road below,
To segashuate wid ole man Joe.

BLACK-EYED PEAS FOR LUCK

ONE time I went a-huntin',
I heared dat 'possum sneeze.
I hollered back to Susan Ann:
"Put on a pot o' peas."

Dat good ole 'lasses candy,
What makes de eyeballs shine,
Wid 'possum peas an' taters,
Is my dish all de time.

* Segashuate means associate with.

† Read first stanza of "Sheep Shell Corn," to know of ole man Joe.

* Dem black-eyed peas is lucky;
When e't on New Year's day,
You always has sweet taters,
An' 'possum come your way.

† PERIWINKLE

PENNYWINKLE, pennywinkle, poke out yō' ho'n;
An' I'll give you five dollahs an' a bar'l o' co'n.
Pennywinkle! Pennywinkle! Dat gal love me?
Jes stick out yō' ho'n all pinted to a tree.

TRAINING THE BOY

W'EN I wus a liddle boy,
Jes thirteen inches high,
I useter climb de table legs,
An' steal off cake an' pie.

Altho' I wus a liddle boy,
An' tho' I wusn't high,
My mammy took dat keen switch down,
An' whupped me till I cry.

* This last stanza embodies one of the old superstitions.

† The Periwinkle seems to have been used as an oracle by some Negroes in the days of their enslavement.

Now I is a great big boy,
An' Mammy, she cain't do it;
My daddy gits a great big stick,
An' pulls me right down to it.

Dey say: "No breakin' dishes now;
No stealin' an' no lies."
An' since I is a great big boy,
Dey 'spects me to act wise.

* BAT! BAT!

Bat! Bat! Come un'er my hat,
An' I'll give you a slish o' bacon.
But don't bring none yō' ole bedbugs,
If you don't want to git fersaken.

RANDSOME TANTSOME

Randsome Tantsome!—Gwine to de Fair?
Randsome Tantsome!—W'at you gwineter wear?
"Dem shoes an' stockin's I'se bound to wear!"
Randsome Tantsome a-gwine to de Fair.

* A superstition that it is good luck to catch a bat in one's hat if he doesn't get bedbugs by so doing.

ARE YOU CAREFUL?

Is you keerful; w'en you goes down de street,
To see dat yō' cloze looks nice an' neat?
Does you watch yō' liddle step 'long de way,
An' think 'bout dem words dat you say?

RABBIT HASH

Dere wus a big ole rabbit
Dat had a mighty habit
A-settin' in my gyardin,.
An' eatin' all my cabbitch.
I hit 'im wid a mallet,
I tapped 'im wid a maul.
Sich anudder rabbit hash,
You's never tasted 'tall.

WHY THE WOODPECKER'S HEAD IS RED

Bill Dillix say to dat woodpecker bird:
"W'at makes yō' topknot red?"
Says he: "I'se picked in de red-hot sun,
Till it's done burnt my head."

BLESSINGS

The chivalry of the Old South rather demanded that all friends should be invited to partake of the meal, if they chanced to come calling about the time of the meal hour. This ideal also pervaded the lowly slave Negro's cabin. In order that this hospitality might not be abused, the Negroes had a little deterrent story which they told their children. Below are the fancied Blessings asked by the fictitious Negro family, in the story, whose hospitality had been abused.

BLESSING WITH COMPANY PRESENT

Oh Lawd now bless an' bīn' us,
An' put ole Satan 'hīn' us.
Oh let yō' Sperit mīn' us.
Don't let none hongry fīn' us.

BLESSING WITHOUT COMPANY

Oh Lawd have mussy now upon us,
An' keep 'way some our neighbors from us.
For w'en dey all comes down upon us,
Dey eats mōs' all our victuals from us.

ANIMAL PERSECUTORS

I WENT up on de mountain,
To git a bag o' co'n.
Dat coon, he sicked 'is dog on me,
Dat 'possum blowed 'is ho'n.

Dat gobbler up an' laugh at me.
Dat pattridge giggled out.
Dat peacock squall to bust 'is sides,
To see me runnin' 'bout.

FOUR RUNAWAY NEGROES—WHENCE THEY CAME

ONCE fō' runaway Niggers,
Dey met in de road.
An' dey ax one nudder:
Whar dey come from.
Den one up an' say:
"I'se jes come down from Chapel Hill
Whar de Niggers hain't wuked an' never will."

Den anudder up an' say:
"I'se jes come here from Guinea Gall
Whar dey eats de cow up, skin an' all."

Den de nex' Nigger say
Whar he done come from:
  "Dey wuked you night an' day as dey could;
  Dey never had stopped an' dey never would."

De las' Nigger say
Whar he come from:
  "De Niggers all went out to de Ball;
  De thick, de thin, de short, de tall."

But dey'd all please set up,
Jes lak ole Br'er Rabbit
W'en he look fer a dog.
An' keep it in mind,
Whilst dey boasts 'bout deir gals
An' dem t'other things:
  "Dat none deir gals wus lak Sallie Jane,
  Fer dat gal wus sweeter dan sugar cane."

WISE SAYING SECTION

LEARN TO COUNT

NAUGHT'S a naught,
Five's a figger.
All fer de white man,
None fer de Nigger.

Ten's a ten,
But it's mighty funny;
When you cain't count good,
You hain't got no money.

THE WAR IS ON

DE boll-weevil's in de cotton,
De cut-worm's in de corn,
De Devil's in de white man;
An' de wah's a-gwine on.
Poor Nigger hain't got no home!
Poor Nigger hain't got no home!

HOW TO PLANT AND CULTIVATE SEEDS

PLANT: One fer de blackbird
Two fer de crow,
Three fer de jaybird
An' fō' fer to grow.

Den: When you goes to wuk,
Don't never stand still;
When you pull de grass,
Pull it out'n de hill.

A MAN OF WORDS

A MAN o' words an' not o' deeds,
Is lak a gyarden full o' weeds.
De weeds 'gin to grow
Lak a gyarden full o' snow.
De snow 'gin to fly
Lak a eagle in de sky.
De sky 'gin to roar
Lak a hammer on yō' door.
De door 'gin to crack
Lak a hick'ry on yō' back.

Yō' back 'gin to smart
Lak a knife in yō' heart.
Yō' heart 'gin to fail
Lak a boat widout a sail.
De boat 'gin to sink
Lak a bottle full o' ink.
Dat ink, it won't write
Neider black nor white.
Dat man o' words an' not o' deeds,
Is lak a gyardėn full o' weeds.

INDEPENDENT

I'SE jes as innerpenunt as a pig on ice.
Gwineter git up ag'in if I slips down twice.
If I cain't git up, I can jes lie down.
I don't want no Niggers to be he'pin' me 'roun'.

TEMPERANCE RHYME

WHISKY nor brandy hain't no friend to my kind.
Dey killed my pō' daddy, an' dey troubled my mind.
Sometime he drunk whisky, sometime he drunk ale;
Sometime he kotch de rawhide, an' sometime de flail.

On yon'er high mountain, I'll set up dar high;
An' de wild geese can cheer me while passin' on by.
Go 'way, young ladies, an' let me alone;
For you know I'se a poor boy, an' a long ways from
home.

Go put up de hosses an' give 'em some hay;
But don't give me no whisky, so long as I stay.
For whisky nor brandy hain't friend to my kind;
Dey killed my pō' daddy, an' dey troubled my mind.

THAT HYPOCRITE

I TELL you how dat hypocrite do,
He come down to my house, an' talk about you;
He talk about me, an' he talk about you;
An' dat's de way dat hypocrite do.

I tell you how dat hypocrite pray.
He pray out loud in de hypocrite way.
He pray out loud, got a heap to say;
An' dat's de way dat hypocrite pray.

I tell you how dat hypocrite 'ten',
He 'ten' dat he love, an' he don't love men.
He 'ten' dat he love, an' he hate Br'er Ben;
An' dat's de way dat hypocrite 'ten'.

DRINKING RAZOR SOUP

He's been drinkin' razzer soup;
Dat sharp Nigger, black lak ink.
If he don't watch dat tongue o' his,
Somebody'll hurt 'im 'fōr' he think.

He cain't drive de pigeons t' roost,
Dough he talk so big an' smart.
Hain't got de sense to tole 'em in.
Cain't more 'an drive dat ole mule chyart.

OLD MAN KNOW-ALL

Ole man Know-All, he come 'round
Wid his nose in de air, turned 'way frum de ground.
His ole woolly head hain't been combed fer a week;
It say: "Keep still, while Know-All speak."

Ole man Know-All's tongue, it run;
He jes know'd ev'rything under de sun.
When you knowed one thing, he knowed mō'.
He 'us sharp 'nough to stick an' green 'nough to
grow.

Ole man Know-All died las' week.
He got drowned in de middle o' de creek.
De bridge wus dar, an' dar to stay.
But he knowed too much to go dat way.

FED FROM THE TREE OF KNOWLEDGE

I NEBBER starts to break my colt,
Till he's ole enough to trabble.
I nebber digs my taters up
W'en dey's only right to grabble.
So w'en you sees me risin' up
To structify in meetin',
You can know I'se climbed de Knowledge
Tree
An' done some apple eatin'.

THE TONGUE

GOT a tongue dat jes run when it walk?
It cain't talk.
Got a tongue dat can hush when it talk?—
It cain't squawk.

BRAG AND BOAST

Brag is a big dog;
But Hold Fast, he is better.
Dem big black rough hands,
Dey cain't write no letter.

Boast, he barks an' growls loud;
But Bulger, he hain't no shirker.
Dat big loud mouf Nigger,
He hain't never no worker.

SELF-CONTROL

Befo' you says dat ugly word,
You stop an' count ten.
Den if you wants to say dat word,
Begin an' count again.

Don't have a tongue tied in de middle,
An' loose frum en' to en'.
You mus' think twice, den speak once;
Dat * donkey cain't count ten.

* The somewhat less dignified term was more commonly used.

SPEAK SOFTLY

"Wus dat you spoke,
Or a fence rail broke?"
Br'er Rabbit say to de Jay
* W'en you don't speak sof',
Yō' baits comes off;
An' de fish jes swim away.

STILL WATER RUNS DEEP

DAT still water, it run deep.
Dat shaller water prattle.
Dat tongue, hung in a holler head,
Jes roll 'round an' rattle.

DON'T TELL ALL YOU KNOW

KEEP dis in min', an' all 'll go right;
As on yō' way you goes;
Be shore you knows 'bout all you tells,
But don't tell all you knows.

* The last three lines of the rhyme was a superstition current among antebellum Negroes.

*JACK AND DINAH WANT FREEDOM

OLE Aunt Dinah, she's jes lak me.
She wuk so hard dat she want to be free.
But, you know, Aunt Dinah's gittin' sorter ole;
An' she's feared to go to Canada, caze it's so cōl'.

Dar wus ole Uncle Jack, he want to git free.
He find de way Norf by de moss on de tree.
He cross dat † river a-floatin' in a tub.
Dem ‡ Patterollers give 'im a mighty close rub.

Dar is ole Uncle Billy, he's a mighty good Nigger.
He tote all de news to Mosser a little bigger.
When you tells Uncle Billy, you wants free fer a fac';
De nex' day de hide drap off'n yō' back.

*The writer wishes to give explanation as to why the rhyme "Jack and Dinah Want Freedom" appears under the Section of Psycho-composite Rhymes as set forth in "The Study——" of our volume. The Negroes repeating this rhyme did not always give the names Jack, Dinah, and Billy, as we here record them, but at their pleasure put in the individual name of the Negro in their surroundings whom the stanza being repeated might represent. Thus this little rhyme was the scientific dividing, on the part of the Negroes themselves, of the members of their race into three general classes with respect to the matter of Freedom.

† The Ohio River.

‡ White guards who caught and kept slaves at the master's home.

FOREIGN SECTION

AFRICAN RHYMES

The rhymes "Tuba Blay," "Near Waldo Tee-do O mah nah mejai," "Sai Boddeoh Sumpun Komo," and "Byanswahn-Byanswahn" were kindly contributed by Mr. John H. Zeigler, Monrovia, Liberia, and Mr. C. T. Wardoh of the Bassa Tribe, Liberia. They are natives and are now in America for collegiate study and training.

NEAR-WALDO-TEE-DO O MAH NAH MEJAI

OR

NEAR-WALDO-TEE-DO IS MY SWEETHEART

1. A YEHN me doddoc Near Waldo Tee-do.
Yehn me doddoc o-o seoh-o-o.
Omah nahn mejai Near Waldo Tee-do.
Omah nahn mejai Near Waldo Tee-do.

Translation

Near Waldo Tee-do gave me a suit.
He gave me a suit.
Near Waldo Tee-do is my sweetheart.
Near Waldo Tee-do is my sweetheart.

TUBA BLAY
OR
AN EVENING SONG

1. SEAH o, Tuba blay.
   Tuba blay, Tuba blay.
2. O blay wulna nahn blay.
   Tuba blay, Tuba blay.

Translation

1. Oh please Tuba sing.
   Tuba sing, Tuba sing.
2. Oh sing that song.
   Tuba sing, Tuba sing.

THE OWL

We are indebted for this Baluba rhyme to Dr. and Mrs. William H. Sheppard, pioneer missionaries under the Southern Presbyterian Church. The little production comes from Congo, Africa.

SALA wa mĕn tĕnge, Cimpungelu.
Sala wa mĕn tĕnge, Cimpungelu.
Meme taya wewe, Cimpungelu.
Sala wa mĕn tĕnge, Cimpungelu.

Translation

The dancing owl waves his spread tail feathers.
I'm the owl.
The dancing owl waves his spread tail feathers.
I'm the owl.
I now tell you by my dancing, I'm the owl.
The dancing owl waves his spread tail feathers.
I'm the owl.

SAI BODDEOH SUMPUN KOMO
OR
I AM NOT GOING TO MARRY SUMPUN

1. SAI Sumpun komo.
De Sumpun nenah?
Sumpun se jello jeppo
Boddeoh Sumpun.

2. Sai Sumpun komo.
De Sumpun nenah?
Sumpun auch nahn jehn deddoc.
Boddeoh Sumpun.

Translation

1. I am not going to marry Sumpun.
What has Sumpun done?
Sumpun doesn't live a seafaring life
Boddeoh Sumpun.

2. I am not going to marry Sumpun.
What has Sumpun done?
Sumpun does not support me.
Boddeoh Sumpun.

BYANSWAHN-BYANSWAHN
OR
A BOAT SONG

Ō-Ō BYANSWAHN blay Tanner tee-o-o.
O Byanswahn jekah jubba.
De jo Byanswahn se kah jujah dai.
Ō Byanswahn blay dai Tanner tee-o-o.

Translation

Oh boat, come back to me.
Since you carried my child away,
I have not seen that child.
Oh boat come back to me.

THE TURKEY BUZZARD

Dr. C. C. Fuller: a missionary at Chikore Melsetter, Rhodesia, Africa, was good enough to secure for the compiler this rhyme, written in Chindau, from the Rev. John E. Hatch, also a missionary in South Africa.

Riti, riti, mwana wa rashika.
Ndizo, ndizo kurgya ku wande.
Riti, riti, mwana wa oneka.
Ndizo, ndizo ti wande issu.

Translation

Turkey buzzard, turkey buzzard, your child is lost.
That is all right, the food will be more plentiful.
Turkey buzzard, turkey buzzard, your child is found.
That is all right, we will increase in number.

THE FROGS

The following child's play rhyme in Baluba with its translation was contributed by Mrs. L. G. Sheppard, who was for many years a missionary in Congo, Africa.

CULA, Cula, Kuya kudi Kunyi?
Tuyiya ku cisila wa Baluba.
Tun kuata tua kuesa cinyi?
Tua kudimuka kua musode.

Translation

Frogs, frogs, where are you going?
We are going to the market of the Baluba.
If they catch you, what will they do?
They will turn us all into lizards.

Jamaica Rhyme

BUSCHER GARDEN

This Negro rhyme from rural Jamaica was contributed by Dr. Cecil B. Roddock, a native of that country. The word *Buscher* means an overseer or master of a plantation.

ALL a night, me da watch a brother Wayrum;
Wayrum ina me Buscher garden.
Oh, Brother Wayrum! Wha' a you da do,
To make a me Buscher a catch a you?
Oh a me Buscher, in a me Buscher garden;
Me a beg a me Buscher a pardon!

VENEZUELAN NEGRO RHYMES

These Venezuelan rhymes: "A 'Would be' Immigrant" and "Game Contestant's Song," came to us through the kindness of Mr. J. C. Williams, Caracas, Venezuela, S. A. He is a native of Venezuela.

GAME CONTESTANT'S SONG

We're going to dig!
We're going to dig a sepulcher to bury those regiments.
White Rose Union!
Get yourself in readiness to bury those regiments.
Oh Grentville! * Cici! Cici!
Beat them forever.

Sa your de vrai!
We'll send them a challenge,
To mardi carnival.
Sa your de vrai!!

* Cici = a kind of game.

A "WOULD BE" IMMIGRANT

Conjo Celestine! Oh
He was going to Panama.
Reavay Trinidad!
Celestine Revay, la Grenada!
What d'you think bring Celestine back?
What d'you think bring Celestine back?
What d'you think bring Celestine to me?
Twenty cents for a cup of tea.

Trinidad Negro Rhymes

We are very grateful to Mr. L. A. Brown for his kindness in giving to us the two Venezuelan rhymes which follow. His home is in Princess Town, Trinidad, B. W. I.

UN BELLE MARIE COOLIE
OR
BEAUTIFUL MARIE, THE EAST INDIAN

Un belle Marie Coolie!
Un belle Marie Coolie!
Un belle Marie Coolie!
Vous belle dame, vous belle pour moi.
Papa est un African.
Mamma est un belle Coolie.
Un belle Marie Coolie!
Vous belle dame, vous belle pour moi.

Translation

Beautiful Marie, the East Indian!
Beautiful Marie, the East Indian!

Beautiful Marie, the East Indian!
You beautiful woman, you're good enough
for me.
Papa is an African.
Mamma is a beautiful East Indian.
Beautiful Marie, the East Indian!
You beautiful woman, you're good enough
for me.

A TOM CAT

My father had a big Tom cat,
That tried to play a fiddle.
He struck it here, and he struck it there,
And he struck it in the middle.

PHILIPPINE ISLAND RHYME

The following rhyme came to me through the kindness of Mr. C. W. Ransom, Grand Chain, Ill., U. S. A. Mr. Ransom served three years with the United States Army in the Philippine Islands.

SEE that Monkey up the cocoanut tree,
A-jumpin' an' a-throwin' nuts at me?
El hombre no savoy,
No like such play.
All same to Americano,
No hay diqué.

A STUDY IN NEGRO FOLK RHYMES

THE lore of the American Negro is rich in story, in song, and in Folk rhymes. These stories and songs have been partially recorded, but so far as I know there is no collection of the American Negro Folk Rhymes. The collection in Part I is a compilation of American Negro Folk Rhymes, and this study primarily concerns them; but it was necessary to have a Foreign Section of Rhymes in order to make our study complete. I have therefore inserted a little Foreign Section of African, Venezuelan, Jamaican, Trinidad, and Philippine Negro Rhymes; and along with them have placed the names of the contributors to whom we are under great obligations, as well as to the many others who have given valuable assistance and suggestions in the matter of the American Negro Rhymes recorded.

When critically measured by the laws and usages governing the best English poetry, Negro Folk Rhymes will probably remind readers of the story of the good brother, who arose solemnly in a Christian praise meeting, and thanked God that he had broken all the Commandments, but had kept his religion.

Though decent rhyme is often wanting, and in the case of the "Song to the Runaway Slave," there is no rhyme at all, the rhythm is found almost perfect in all of them.

A few of the Rhymes bear the mark of a somewhat recent date in composition. The majority of them, however, were sung by Negro fathers and mothers in the dark days of American slavery to their children who listened with eyes as large as saucers and drank them down with mouths wide open. The little songs were similar in structure to the Jubilee Songs, also of Negro Folk origin.

If one will but examine the recorded Jubilee songs, he will find that it is common for stanzas, which are apparently most distantly related in structure, to sing along in perfect rhythm in the same tune that carefully counts from measure to measure one, two; or one, two, three, four. Here is an example of two stanzas taken from the Jubilee song, "Wasn't That a Wide River?"

1. "Old Satan's just like a snake in the grass,
   He's a-watching for to bite you as you pass.
2. Shout! Shout! Satan's about.
   Just shut your door, and keep him out."

An examination of stanzas in various Jubilee songs will show in the same song large variations in poetic feet, etc., not only from stanza to stanza; but very often from line to line, and even from phrase to phrase. Notwithstanding all this variation, a well trained band of singers will render the songs with such perfect rhythm that one scarcely realizes that the structure of any one stanza differs materially from that of another.

A stanza, as it appears in Negro Folk Rhymes, is of the same construction as that found in the Jubilee Songs. A perfect rhythm is there. If while reading them you miss it, read yet once again; you will find it in due season if you "faint not" too early.

As a rule, Negro Folk verse is so written that it fits into measures of music written 4/4 or 2/4 time. You can therefore read Negro Folk Rhymes silently counting: one, two; or, one, two, three, four; and the stanzas fit directly into the imaginary music measures if you are reading in harmony with the intended rhythm. I know of only three Jubilee Songs whose stanzas are transcribed as exceptions. They are—

(1) "I'm Going to Live with Jesus," 6/8 time, (2) "Gabriel's Trumpet's Going to Blow," 3/4 time, and (3) "Lord Make Me More Patient," 6/8 time.

It is interesting to note along with these that the "Song of the Great Owl," the "Negro Soldier's Civil War Chant," and "Destitute Former Slave Owners," are seemingly the only ones in our Folk Rhyme collection which would call for a ¾ or 6/8 measure. Such a measure is rare in all literary Negro Folk productions.

The Negro, then, repeated or sang his Folk Rhymes, and danced them to 4/4 and 2/4 measures. Thus Negro Folk Rhymes, with very few exceptions, are poetry where a music measure is the unit of measurement for the words rather than the poetic foot. This is true whether the Rhyme is, or is not, sung. *Imaginary measures either of two or four beats, with a given number of words to a beat, a number that can be varied limitedly at will, seems to be the philosophy underlying all Negro slave rhyme construction.*

As has just been casually mentioned, the Negro Folk Rhyme was used for the dance. There are Negro Folk Rhyme Dance Songs and Negro Folk Dance Rhymes. An example of the former is found in "The Banjo Picking," and of the latter, "Juba," both found in this collection. The reader may wonder how a Rhyme simply repeated was used in the dance. The procedure was as follows: Usually one or two individuals "star" danced at time. The others of the crowd (which was usually large) formed a circle about this one or two who were to take their prominent turn at dancing. I use the terms 'star" danced and "prominent turn" because in the latter part of our study we shall find that all those present engaged sometimes at intervals in the dance. But those forming the circle, for most of the time, repeated the Rhyme, clapping their hands together, and patting their feet in rhythmic time with the words of the Rhyme being repeated. It was the task of the dancers in the middle of the circle to execute some graceful dance in such a manner that their feet would beat a tattoo upon the ground answering to every word, and sometimes to every syllable of the Rhyme being repeated by those in the circle. There were many such Rhymes. " 'Possum Up the Gum Stump," and "Jawbone" are good examples. The stanzas to these Rhymes were not usually limited to two or three, as is generally the case with those recorded in our collection. Each selection usually had many stanzas. Thus as there came variation in the words from stanza to stanza, the skill of the dancers was taxed to its utmost, in order to keep up the graceful dance and to beat a changed tattoo upon the ground corresponding to the changed words. If any find fault with the limited number of stanzas recorded in our treatise, I can in apology only sing the words of a certain little encore song each of whose two little stanzas ends with the words, "Please don't call us back, because we don't know any more."

There is a variety of Dance Rhyme to which it is fitting to call attention. This variety is illustrated in our collection by "Jump Jim Crow," and "Juba." In such dances as these, the dancers were required to give such movements of body as would act the sentiment expressed by the words while keeping up the common requirements of beating these same words in a tattoo upon the ground with the feet and executing simultaneously a graceful dance.

It is of interest also to note that the antebellum Negro while repeating his Rhymes which had no connection with the dance usually accompanied the repeating with the patting of his foot upon the ground. Among other things he was counting off the invisible measures and bars of his Rhymes, things largely unseen by the world but very real to him. Every one who has listened to a well sung Negro Jubilee Song knows that it is almost impossible to hear one sung and not pat the foot. I have seen the feet of the coldest blooded Caucasians pat right along while Jubilee melodies were being sung.

All Negro Folk productions, including the Negro Folk Rhymes, seem to call for this patting of the foot. The explanation which follows is offered for consideration. The orchestras of the Native African were made up largely of crudely constructed drums of one sort or another. Their war songs and so forth were sung to the accompaniment of these drum orchestras. When the Negroes were transported to America, and began to sing songs and to chant words in another tongue, they still sang strains calling, through inheritance, for the accompaniment of their ancestral drum. The Negro's drum having fallen from him as he entered civilization, he unwittingly called into service his foot to take its place. This substitution finds a parallelism in the highly cultivated La France rose, which being without stamens and pistils must be propagated by cuttings or graftings instead of by seeds. The rose, purposeless, emits its sweet perfume to the breezes and thus it attracts insects for cross fertilization simply because its staminate and pistillate ancestors thus called the insect world for that purpose. The rattle of the crude drum of the Native African was loud by inheritance in the hearts of his early American descendants and its unseen ghost walks in the midst of all their poetry.

Many Negro Folk Rhymes were used as banjo and fiddle (violin) songs. It ought to be borne in mind, however, that even these were quite often repeated without singing or playing. It was common in the early days of the public schools of the South to hear Negro children use them as declamations. The connection, however, of Negro Folk Rhymes with their secular music productions is well worthy of notice.

I have often heard those who liked to think and discuss things musical, wonder why little or no music of a secular kind worth while seemed to be found among Negroes while their religious music, the Jubilee Songs, have challenged the admiration of the world. The songs of most native peoples seem to strike "high water mark" in the secular form. Probably numbers of us have heard the explanation: "You see, the Negro is deeply emotional; religion appealed to him as did nothing else. The Negro therefore spent his time singing and shouting praises to God, who alone could whisper in his heart and stir up these emotions." There is perhaps much truth in this explanation. It is also such a delicate and high compliment to the Negro race, that I hesitate to touch it. One of the very few gratifying things that has come to Negroes is the unreserved recognition of their highly religious character. There is a truth, however, about the relation between the Negro Folk Rhyme and the Negro's banjo and fiddle music which ought to be told even though some older, nicer viewpoints might be a little shifted.

There were quite a few Rhymes sung where the banjo and fiddle formed what is termed in music a simple accompaniment. Examples of these are found in "Run, Nigger, Run," and "I'll Wear Me a Cotton Dress." In such cases the music consisted of simple short tunes unquestionably "born to die."

There was another class of Rhymes like "Devilish Pigs," that were used with the banjo and fiddle in quite another way. It was the banjo and fiddle productions of this kind of Rhyme that made the "old time" Negro banjo picker and fiddler famous. It has caused quite a few, who heard them, to declare that, saint or sinner, it was impossible to keep your feet still while they played. The compositions were comparatively long. From one to four lines of a Negro Folk Rhyme were sung to the opening measures of the instrumental composition; then followed the larger and remaining part of the composition, instruments alone. In the Rhyme "Devilish Pigs" four lines were used at a time. Each time that the music theme of the composition was repeated, another set of Rhyme lines was repeated; and the variations in the music theme were played in each repeat which recalled the newly repeated words of the Rhyme. The ideal in composition from an instrumental viewpoint might quite well remind one of the ideal in piano compositions, which consists of a theme with variations. The first movement of Beethoven's Sonata, Opus 26, illustrates the music ideal in composition to which I refer.

So far as I know no Caucasian instrumental music composer has ever ordered the performers under his direction to sing a few of the first measures of his composition while the string division of the orchestra played its opening chords. Only the ignorant Negro composer has done this. Some white composers have made little approaches to it. A fair sample of an approach is found in the Idylls of Edward McDowell, for piano, where every exquisite little tone picture is headed by some gem in verse, reading which the less musically gifted may gain a deeper insight into the philosophical tone discourse set forth in the notes and chords of the composition.

The Negro Folk Rhyme, then, furnished the ideas

about which the "old time" Negro banjo picker and fiddler clustered his best instrumental music thoughts. It is too bad that this music passed away unrecorded save by the hearts of men. Paul Laurence Dunbar depicts its telling effects upon the hearer in his poem "The Party":

"Cripple Joe, de ole rheumatic, danced dat flo' frum side to middle.
Throwed away his crutch an' hopped it, what's rheumatics 'gainst a fiddle?
Eldah Thompson got so tickled dat he lak to los' his grace,
Had to take bofe feet an' hold 'em, so's to keep 'em in deir place.
An' de Christuns an' de sinnahs got so mixed up on dat flo',
Dat I don't see how dey's pahted ef de trump had chonced to blow."

Perhaps a new school of orchestral music might be built on the Negro idea that some of the performers sing a sentence or so here and there, both to assist the hearers to a clearer musical understanding and to heighten the general artistic finish. The old Negro performers generally sang lines of the Folk Rhymes at the opening but occasionally in the midst of their instrumental compositions. I do not recall any case where lines were sung to the closing measures of the compositions.

It might seem odd to some that the grotesque Folk Rhyme should have given rise to comparatively long instrumental music compositions. I think the explanation is probably very simple. The African on his native heath had his crude ancestral drum as his leading musical instrument. He sang or shouted his war songs consisting of a few words, and of a few notes, then followed them up with the beating of his drum, perhaps for many minutes, or even for hours. In civilization, the banjo, fiddle, "quills," and "triangle" largely took the place of his drum. Thus the singing of opening strains and following them with the main body of the instrumental composition, is in keeping with the Negro's inherited law for instrumental compositions from his days of savagery. The rattling, distinct tones of the banjo, recalling unconsciously his inherited love for the rattle of the African ancestral drum, is probably the thing which caused that instrument to become a favorite among Negro slaves.

I would next consider the relation of the Folk Rhymes to Negro child life. They were instilled into children as warnings. In the years closely following our Civil War, it was common for a young Negro child, about to engage in a doubtful venture, to hear his mother call out to him the Negro Rhyme recorded by Joel Chandler Harris, in the Negro story, "The End of Mr. Bear":

"Tree stan' high, but honey mighty sweet—
Watch dem bees wid stingers on der feet."

These lines commonly served to recall the whole story, it being the Rabbit's song in that story, and the child stopped whatever he was doing. Other and better examples of such Rhymes are 'Young Master and Old Master," "The Alabama Way," and "You Had Better Mind Master," found in our collection.

The warnings were commonly such as would help the slave to escape more successfully the lash, and to live more comfortably under slave conditions. I would not for once intimate that I entertain the thought that the ignorant slave carefully and philosophically studied his surroundings, reasoned it to be a fine method to warn children through poetry, composed verse, and like a wise man proceeded to use it. Of course thinking preceded the making of the Rhyme, but a conscious system of making verses for the purpose did not exist. I have often watched with interest a chicken hen lead forth her brood of young for the first time. While the scratching and feeding are going on, all of a sudden the hen utters a loud shriek, and flaps her wings. The little chicks, although they have never seen a hawk, scurry hither and thither, and so prostrate their little brown and ashen bodies upon the ground as almost to conceal themselves. The Negro Folk Rhymes of warning must be looked upon a little in this same light. They are but the strains of terror given by the promptings of a mother instinct full enough of love to give up life itself for its defenseless own.

Many Rhymes were used to convey to children the common sense truths of life, hidden beneath their comic, crudely cut coats. Good examples are "Old Man Know-All," "Learn to Count," and "Shake the Persimmons Down." All through the Rhymes will be found here and there many stanzas full of common uncommon sense, worthwhile for children.

Many Negro Folk Rhymes repeated or sung to children on their parents' knees were enlarged and told to them as stories, when they became older. The Rhyme in our collection on "Judge Buzzard" is one of this kind. In the Negro version of the race between the hare and the tortoise ("rabbit and terrapin"), the tortoise wins not through the hare's going to sleep, but through a gross deception of all concerned, including even the buzzard who acted as Judge. The Rhyme is a laugh on "Jedge Buzzard." It was commonly repeated to Negro children in olden days when they passed erroneous judgments. "Buckeyed rabbit! Whoopee!" in our volume belongs with the Negro story recorded by Joel Chandler Harris under the title, "How Mr. Rabbit Lost His Fine Bushy Tail," though for some reason Mr. Harris failed to weave it into the story as was the Negro custom. "The Turtle's Song," in our collection, is another, which belongs with the story, "Mr. Terrapin Shows His Strength"; a Negro story given to the world by the same author, though the Rhyme was not recorded by him. It might be of interest to know that the Negroes, when themselves telling the Folk stories, usually sang the Folk Rhyme portions to little "catchy" Negro tunes. I would not under any circumstances intimate that Mr. Harris carelessly left them out. He recorded many little stanzas in the midst of the stories. Examples are:

(a) "We'll stay at home when you're away
'Cause no gold won't pay toll."

(b) "Big bird catch, little bird sing.
Bug bee zoom, little bee sting.
Little man lead, and the big horse follow,
Can you tell what's good for a head in a hollow?"

These and many others are fragmentarily recorded among Mr. Harris' Negro stories in "Nights With Uncle Remus."

Folk Rhymes also formed in many cases the words of Negro Play Songs. "Susie Girl," and "Peep Squirrel," found in our collection, are good illustrations of the Rhymes used in this way. The words and the music of such Rhymes were usually of poor quality. When, however, they were sung by children with the proper accompanying body movements, they might quite well remind one of the "Folk Dances" used in the present best up-to-date Primary Schools. They were the little rays of sunshine in the dark dreary monotonous lives of black slave children.

Possibly the thing which will impress the reader most in reading Negro Folk Rhymes is their good-natured drollery and sparkling nonsense. I believe this is very important. Many have recounted in our hearing, the descriptions of "backwoods" Negro picnics. I have witnessed some of them where the good-natured vender of lemonade and cakes cried out:

"Here's yō' cōl' ice lemonade,
It's made in de shade,
It's stirred wid a spade.
Come buy my cōl' ice lemonade.
It's made in de shade
An' sōl' in de sun.
Ef you hain't got no money,
You cain't git none.
One glass fer a nickel,
An' two fer a dime,
Ef you hain't got de chink,
You cain't git mine.
Come right dis way,
Fer it shō' will pay
To git candy fer de ladies
An' cakes fer de babies."

"Did these venders sell?" Well, all agree that they did. The same principle applied, with much of the nonsense eliminated, will probably make of the Negro a great merchant, as caste gives way enough to allow him a common man's business chance. Of all the races of men, the Negro alone has demonstrated his ability to come into contact with the white man and neither move on nor be annihilated. I believe this is largely due to his power to muster wit and humor on all occasions, and even to laugh in the face of adversity. He refused during the days of slavery to take the advice of Job's wife, and to "Curse God and die." He repeated and sang his comic Folk Rhymes, danced, lived, and came out of the Night of Bondage comparatively strong.

The compiler of the Rhymes was quite interested to find that as a rule the country-reared Negro had a larger acquaintance with Folk Rhymes than one brought up in the city. The human mind craves occasional recreation, entertainment, and amusement. In cities where there is an almost continuous passing along the crowded thoroughfares of much that contributes to these ends, the slave Negro needed only to keep his eyes open, his ears attentive, and laugh. He directed his life accordingly. But, in the country districts there was only the monotony of quiet woods and waving fields of cotton. The rural scenes, though beautiful in themselves, refuse to amuse or entertain those who will not hold communion with them. The country Negro longing for amusement communed in his crude way, and Nature gave him Folk Rhymes for entertainment. Among those found to be clearly of this kind may be mentioned "The Great Owl's Song," "Tails," "Redhead Woodpecker," "The Snail's Reply," "Bobwhite's Song," "Chuck Will's Widow Song," and many others.

The Folk Rhymes were not often repeated as such or as whole compositions by the "grown-ups" among Negroes apart from the Play and the Dance. If, however, you had had an argument with an antebellum Negro, had gotten the better of the argument, and he still felt confident that he was right, you probably would have heard him close his side of the debate with the words: "Well, 'Ole Man Know-All is Dead.'" This is only a short prosaic version of his rhyme "Old Man Know-All," found in our collection. Many of the characteristic sayings of "Uncle Remus" woven into story by Joel Chandler Harris had their origin in these Folk Rhymes. "Dem dat know too much sleep under de ash-hopper" (Uncle Remus) clearly intimates to all who know about the old-fashioned ash-hopper that such an individual lies. This saying is a part of another stanza of "Old Man Know-All," but I cannot recall it from my dim memory of the past, and others whom I have asked seem equally unable to do so, though they have once known it.

As is the case with all things of Folk origin,

there is usually more than one version of each Negro Folk Rhyme. In many cases the exercising of a choice between many versions was difficult. I can only express the hope that my choices have been wise.

There are two American Negro Folk Rhymes in our collection: "Frog in a Mill" and "Tree Frogs," which are oddities in "language." They are rhymes of a rare type of Negro, which has long since disappeared. They were called "Ebo" Negroes and "Guinea" Negroes. The so-called "Ebo" Negro used the word "la" very largely for the word "the." This and some other things have caused me to think that the "Ebo" Negro was probably one who was first a slave among the French, Spanish, or Portuguese, and was afterwards sold to an English-speaking owner. Thus his language was a mixture of African, English, and one of these languages. The so-called "Guinea" Negro was simply one who had not been long from Africa; his language being a mixture of his African tongue and English. These rhymes are to the ordinary Negro rhymes what "Jutta Cord la in'"Nights with Uncle Remus," by Joel Chandler Harris, is to the ordinary Negro stories found there. They are probably representative, in language, of the most primitive Negro Folk productions.

Some of the rhymes are very old indeed. If one

will but read "Master Is Six Feet One Way," found in our collection, he will find in it a description of a slave owner attired in Colonial garb. It clearly belongs, as to date of composition, either to Colonial days, or to the very earliest years of the American Republic. When we consider it as a slave rhyme, it is far from crudest, notwithstanding the early period of its production.

If one carefully studies our collection of rhymes, he will probably get a new and interesting picture of the Negro's mental attitude and reactions during the days of his enslavement. One of these mental reactions is calculated to give one a surprise. One would naturally expect the Negro under hard, trying, bitter slave conditions, to long to be white. There is a remarkable Negro Folk rhyme which shows that this was not the case. This rhyme is: "I'd Rather Be a Negro Than a Poor White Man." We must bear in mind that a Folk Rhyme from its very nature carries in it the crystallized thought of the masses. This rhyme, though a little acidic and though we have recorded the milder version, leaves the unquestioned conclusion that, though the Negro masses may have wished for the exalted station of the rich Southern white man and possibly would have willingly had a white color as a passport to position, there never was a time when the Negro masses desired to be white for the sake of being white. Of course there is the Negro rhyme, "I Wouldn't Marry a Black Girl," but along with it is another Negro rhyme, "I Wouldn't Marry a White or a Yellow Negro Girl." The two rhymes simply point out together a division of Negro opinion as to the ideal standard of beauty in personal complexion. One part of the Negroes thought white or yellow the more beautiful standard and the other part of the Negroes thought black the more beautiful standard.

The body of the Rhymes, here and there, carries many facts between the lines, well worth knowing.

This collection also will shed some light on how the Negro managed to go through so many generations "in slavery and still come out" with a bright, capable mind. There were no colleges or schools for them, but there were Folk Rhymes, stories, Jubilee songs, and Nature; they used these and kept mentally fit.

I now approach the more difficult and probably the most important portion of my discussion in the Study of Negro Folk Rhymes. It is a discussion that I would have willingly omitted, had I not thought that some one owed it to the world. Seeing a debt, as I thought, and not seeing another to pay it, I have reluctantly undertaken to discharge the obligation.

If I were so fortunate as to possess a large flower garden with many new and rare genera and species, and wished to acquaint my friends with them, I should first take these friends for a walk through the garden, that they might see the odd tints and hues, might inhale a little of the new fragrance, and might get some idea as to the prospects for the utilization of these new plants in the world. Then, taking these friends back to my study room, I should consider in a friendly manner along with them, the Families and the Species, and the varieties. Finally, I should endeavor to lay before them from whence these new and strange flowers came. I have endeavored to pursue this method in my discussion of the Negro Folk Rhymes. In the foregoing I have endeavored to take the friendly reader for a walk through this new and strange garden of Rhymes, and I now extend an invitation to him to come into the Study Room for a more critical view of them.

When one enters upon the slightest contemplation of Negro Folk Rhyme classification, and is kind-hearted enough to dignify them with a claim to kinship to real poetry, the word *Ballad* rolls out without the slightest effort, as a term that takes them all in. Yes, this is very true, but they are of a strange type indeed. They are Nature Ballads, many of them, in the sense as ordinarily used. In quite another sense, however, from that in which Nature Ballad is ordinarily used, about all Folk Rhymes are Nature Ballads.

I do not have reference to the thought content, but have reference to what I term Nature Ballads in form. Permit me to explain by analogy just what I would convey by the term Nature Ballad in form.

All Nature is one. Though we arbitrarily divide Nature's objects for study, they are indissolubly bound together and every part carries in some part of its constitution some well defined marks which characterize the other parts with which it has no immediate connection. To illustrate: the absolutely pure sapphire, pure aluminic oxide, crystallized, is commonly colorless, but we know that Nature's most beautiful sapphires are not colorless, but are blue, and of other beautiful tints. These color tints are due to minutest traces of other substances, not at all of general common sapphire composition. We call them all sapphires, however, regardless of their little impurities which are present to enhance their charm and beauty. Likewise, all animal life begins with one cell, and though the one cell in one case develops into a vertebrate, and in another case into an invertebrate the cells persist and so all animal life has cellular structure in common. Yet, each animal branch has predominant traits that distinguish it from all other branches. This same thing is true of plants.

Nature's method, then, of making things seems to be to put in a large enough amount of one thing to brand the article, and then to mix in, in small amounts, enough of other things to lend charm and beauty without taking the article out of its general class.

This is that which goes to make Negro Folk Rhymes Nature Ballads in form. They are ballads, but all in the midst of even a Dance Song, by Nature an ordinary ballad, there may be interwoven comedy, tragedy, and nearly every kind of imaginable thing which goes rather with other general forms of poetry than with the ballad. As an example, in the Dance Song, "Promises of Freedom," we have mustered before our eyes the comic drawing of a deceptive ugly old Mistress and then follows the intimation of the tragic death of a poisoned slave owner, and as we are tempted to dance along in thought with the rhymer, we cannot escape getting the subtle impression that this slave had at least some "vague" personal knowledge of how the Master got that poison. It is a common easy-going ballad, but it is tinted with tragedy and comedy. This general principle will be found to run very largely through the highest types of Negro Folk Rhymes. It is the Nature method of construction, and thus we call them Nature Ballads in structure, or form.

Other good examples of rhymes, Nature Ballads in structure, are "Frog Went a-Courting," "Sheep Shell Corn," "Jack and Dinah Want Freedom."

I now direct attention further to the classification of Negro Rhymes as Ballads. My earnest desire was to classify Negro Rhymes under ordinary headings such as are used by literary men and women everywhere in their general classification of Ballads. I considered this very important because it would enable students of comparative Literature to compare easily the Negro Folk Rhymes with the Folk Rhymes of all peoples. I was much disappointed when I found that the Negro Folk Rhymes, when invited, refused to take their places whole-heartedly in the ordinary classification. As an example of many may be mentioned the little Rhyme "Jaybird." It is a Dance Song, and thus comes under the Dance Song Division, commonly used for Ballads. But, it also belongs under Nature Lore heading, because the Negroes many years ago often told a story, in conjunction with song, of the great misfortunes which overtook a Negro who tried to get his living by hunting Jaybirds. Finally it also belongs under the heading Superstitions, for its last stanza very plainly alludes to the old Negro superstition of slavery days which declared that it was almost impossible to find Jaybirds on Friday because they went to Hades on that day to carry sand to the Devil.

But so important do I think of comparative study that I have taken the ordinary headings used for Ballads and, after adding that omnibus heading "Miscellaneous," have done my best. The majority of the Rhymes can be placed under headings ordinarily used. This was to be expected. It is in obedience to Natural Law. We see it in the Music World. The Caucasian music has eight fundamental tones, the Japanese music has five, while, according to some authorities, Negro Jubilee-music has nine; yet all these music scales have five tones in common. In the Periodic System of Elements there are two periods; a short period and a long period, but both periods embrace, in common, elements belonging to the same family. So with the Ballads, certain classification headings will very well take in both the Negro and all others. The Negro

Ballad, however, does not entirely properly fit in. I have therefore resorted to the following expedient: I have taken the headings ordinarily used, and have listed under each heading the Negro Rhymes which belong with it, as nearly as possible. I have placed this classified list at the end of the book, under the title "Comparative Study Index." By using this Index one can locate and compare Negro Folk productions with the corresponding Folk productions of other peoples.

The headings found in this Comparative Study Index are as follows:

1. Love Songs.
2. Dance Songs.
3. Animal and Nature Lore.
4. Nursery Rhymes.
5. Charms and Superstitions.
6. Hunting Songs.
7. Drinking Songs.
8. Wise and Gnomic Sayings.
9. Harvest Songs.
10. Biblical and Religious Themes.
11. Play Songs.
12. Miscellaneous.

With the way paved for others to make such comparative study as they would like, I now feel free to use a classification which lends itself more easily to a discussion of the origin and evolution of Negro Rhyme. The basic principle used in this classification is Origin and under each source of origin is placed the various classes of Rhymes produced. It has seemed to the writer, who is himself a Negro, and has spent his early years in the midst of the Rhymes and witnessed their making, that there are three great divisions derived from three great mainsprings or sources.

The Divisions are as follows:

I. Rhymes derived from the Social Instinct.

II. Rhymes derived from the Homing Instinct.

III. Rhymes of Psycho-composite origin.

The terms Social and Homing Instincts are familiar to every one, but the term Psycho-composite was coined by the writer after much hesitation and with much regret because he seemed unable to find a word which would express what he had in mind.

To make clear: the classes of Rhymes falling under Divisions I and II owe their crudest initial beginnings to instinct, while those under Division III owe their crudest beginnings partly to instinct, but partly also to intelligent thinking processes. To illustrate—Courtship Rhymes come under Division II, because courtship primarily arises from the homing instinct, but when we come to "quasi" wise sayings—directed largely to criticism or toward improvement, there is very much more than instinct concerned. In Division III the Rhymes are directed largely to improvement. In explanation of why they are in Division III, I would say, the desire to better one's condition is instinctive, but the slightest attainment of the desire comes through thought pure and simple. I have invented the term Psycho-composite to include all this.

In reading the Rhymes under Division III, one finds comparatively large, abstract, general conclusions, such as—General loquaciousness is unwise: Assuming to know everything is foolish: Self-control is a great virtue. Proper preparation must be made before presuming to give instruction, etc. Such generalizations involve something not necessarily present in the crudest initiations of such Rhymes as those found under Divisions I and II. Below is a tabular view of my proposed classification of Negro Folk Rhymes:

Division	Class
I. Social Instinct Rhymes	1. Dance Rhymes
	2. Dance Rhyme Songs
	3. Play Songs
	4. Pastime Rhymes

Division	Class
II. Homing Instinct Rhymes	1. Love Rhymes 2. Courtship Rhymes 3. Marriage Rhymes 4. Married Life Rhymes
III. Psycho-composite Rhymes	1. Criticism and Improvement Rhymes

Under this tabulation, let us now proceed to discuss the Origin and Evolution of Negro Folk Rhymes.

Early in my discussion the reader will recall that I explained in considerable detail how the Dance Rhyme words were used in the dance. I am now ready to announce that the Dance Rhyme was derived from the dance, and to explain how the Dance Rhyme became an evolved product of the dance.

I witnessed in my early childhood the making of a few Dance Rhymes. I have forgotten the words of most of those whose individual making I witnessed but the "Jonah's Band Party" found in our collection is one whose making I distinctly recall. I shall tell in some detail of its origin because it serves in a measure to illustrate how the Dance Rhymes probably had their beginnings. First of all be it known that there was a "step" in dancing, originated by some Negro somewhere, called "Jonah's Band" step. There is no need that I should try to describe that step which, though of the plain dance type, was accompanied from the beginning to the end by indescribable "frills" of foot motion. I can't describe it, but if one will take a stick and cause it to tap so as to knock the words: "Setch a kickin' up san'! Jonah's band," while he repeats the words in the time of 2/4 music measure, the taps will reproduce the tattoo beaten upon the ground by the feet of the dancers, when they danced the "Jonah's Band" step. The dancers formed a circle placing two or more of their skilled dancers in the middle of it. Now when I first witnessed this dance, there were no words said at all. There was simply patting with the hands and dancing, making a tattoo which might be well represented by the words supplied later on in its existence. Later, I witnessed the same dance, where the patting and dancing were as usual, but one man, apparently the leader, was simply crying out the words, "Setch a kickin' up san'!" and the crowd answered with the words, "Jonah's Band!"—the words all being repeated in rhythmic harmony with the patting and dancing. Thus was born the line, "Setch a kickin' up san'! Jonah's Band!" In some places it was the custom to call on the dancers to join with those of the circle, at intervals in the midst of the dance, in dancing other steps than the Jonah's Band step. Some dance leaders, for example, simply called in plain prose—"Dance the Mobile Buck," others calling for another step would rhyme their call. Thus arose the last lines to each stanza, such as—

"Raise yō' right foot, kick it up high!
Knock dat 'Mobile Buck' in de eye!"

This is the genesis of the "Jonah's Band Party," found in our collection. The complete rhyme becomes a fine description of an old-time Negro party. It is probable that much Dance Rhyme making originated in this or a similar way.

Let us assume that Negro customs in Slavery days were what they were in my childhood days, then it would come about that such an ocasional Rhyme making in a crowd would naturally stimulate individual Rhyme makers, and from these individuals would naturally grow up "crops" of Dance Rhymes. Of course I cannot absolutely know, but I think when I witnessed the making of the "Jonah's Band Party," that I witnessed the stimulus which had produced the Dance Rhyme through the decades of preceding years. I realize, however, that this does not account for the finished Rhyme products. It simply gives one source of origin. How the Rhyme grew to its complex structure will be discussed later, because that discussion belongs not to the Dance Rhyme alone, but to all the Rhymes.

There was a final phase of development of "Jonah's Band Party" witnessed by the writer; namely, the singing of the lines, "Setch a kickin' up san'! Jonah's Band!" The last lines of the stanzas, the lines calling for another step on the part of both the circle and the dancers, were never sung to my knowledge. The little tune to the first lines consisted of only four notes, and is inserted below.

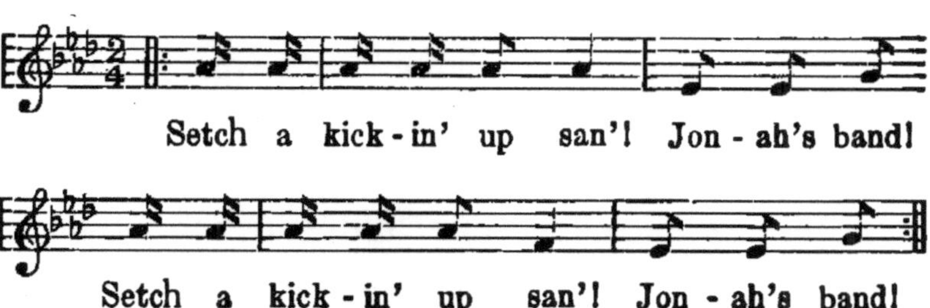

I give this as of interest because it marks a partial transition from a Dance Rhyme to a Dance Rhyme Song. In days of long ago I occasionally saw a Dance Rhyme Song "patted and danced" instead of sung or played and danced. This coupled with the transition stage of the "Jonah's Band Dance"

just given has caused me to believe that Dance Rhyme Songs were probably evolved from Dance Rhymes pure and simple, through individuals putting melodies to these Dance Rhymes.

As Dance Rhymes came from the dance, so likewise Play Rhymes came from plays. I shall now discuss the one found in our collection under the caption—"Goosie-gander." Since the Play has probably passed from the memory of most persons, I shall tell how it was played. The children (and sometimes those in their teens) sat in a circle. One individual, the leader, walked inside the circle, from child to child, and said to each in turn, "Goosie-gander." If the child answered "Goose," the leader said, "I turn your ears loose," and went on to the next child. If he answered "Gander," the leader said, "I pull yō' years 'way yander." Then ensued a scuffle between the two children; each trying to pull the other's ears. The fun for the circle came from watching the scuffle. Finally the child who got his ears pulled took his place in the circle, leaving the victor as master of ceremonies to call out the challenge "Goosie-gander!" The whole idea of the play is borrowed from the fighting of the ganders of a flock of geese for their mates. Many other plays were likewise borrowed from Nature. Examples are found in "Hawk and Chickens Play," and "Fox and Geese Play." "Caught by a Witch Play" is borrowed from superstition. But to return to "Goosie-gander"—most children of our childhood days played it, using common prose in the calls, and answers just as we have here described it. A few children here and there so gave their calls and responses as to rhyme them into a kind of a little poem as it is recorded in our collection. Without further argument, I think it can hardly be doubted that the whole thing began as a simple prose call, and response, and that some child inclined to rhyming things, started "to do the rest," and was assisted in accomplishing the task by other children equally or more gifted. This reasonably accounts for the origin of the Play Rhyme.

Now what of the Play Rhyme Songs? There were many more Play Rhyme Songs than Play Rhymes. There were some of the Play Rhyme Songs sung in prose version by some children and the same Play Song would be sung in rhymed version by other children. Likewise the identical Play Song would not be sung at all by other children; they would simply repeat the words as in the case of the Rhyme "Goosie-gander," just discussed. The little Play Song found in our collection under the caption, "Did You Feed My Cow?" is one which was current in my childhood in the many versions as just indicated. The general thought in the story of the Rhyme was the same in all versions whether prose or rhyme, or song. In cases where children repeated it instead of singing it, it was generally in prose and the questions were so framed by the leader that all the general responses by the crowd were "Yes, Ma'am!" Where it was sung, it was invariably rhymed; and the version found in this collection was about the usual one.

The main point in the discussion at this juncture is—that there were large numbers of Play Songs like this one found in the transition stage from plain prose to repeated rhyme, and to sung rhyme. Such a status leaves little doubt that the Play Song travelled this general road in its process of evolution.

I might take up the Courtship Rhymes, and show that they are derivatives of Courtship, and so on to the end of all the classes given in my outline, but since the evidences and arguments in all the cases are essentially the same I deem it unnecessary.

I now turn attention to a peculiar general ideal in Form found in Negro Folk Rhymes. It probably is not generally known that the Negroes, who emerged from the House of Bondage in the 60's of the last century, had themselves given a name to their own peculiar form of verse. If it be known I am rather confident that it has never been written. They named the parts of their verse "Call," and (Re) "Sponse." After explaining what is meant by 'call' and "sponse," I shall submit an evidence on the matter. In its simplest form "call" and "sponse" were what we would call in Caucasian music, solo and chorus. As an example, in the little Play Song used in our illustration of Play Songs, "Did You Feed My Cow?" was sung as a solo and was known as the "Call," while the chorus that answered "Yes, Ma'am" was known as the "Sponse."

I now beg to offer testimony in corroboration of my assertion that Negroes had named their Rhyme parts "Call" and "Sponse." So well were these established parts of a Negro Rhyme recognized among Negroes that the whole turning point of one of their best stories was based upon it. I have reference to the Negro story recorded by Mr. Joel Chandler Harris in his "Nights with Uncle Remus," under the caption, "Brother Fox, Brother Rabbit, and King Deer's Daughter." Those who would enjoy the story, as the writer did in his childhood days, as it fell from the lips of his dear little friends and dusky playmates, will read the story in Mr.

Harris' book. The gist of the story is as follows: The fox and the rabbit fall in love with King Deer's daughter. The fox has just about become the successful suitor, when the rabbit goes through King Deer's lot and kills some of King Deer's goats. He then goes to King Deer, and tells him that the fox killed the goats, and offers to make the fox admit the deed in King Deer's hearing. This being agreed to, the rabbit goes to find the fox, and proposes that they serenade the King Deer family. The fox agreed. Then the rabbit proposes that he sing the "Call" and that the fox sing the "Sponse" (or, as Mr. Harris records the story, the "answer"), and this too was agreed upon. We now quote from Mr. Harris:

"Ole Br'er Rabbit, he make up de song he own se'f en' he fix it so that he sing de *Call* lak de Captain er de co'n-pile, en ole Br'er Fox, he hatter sing de answer" . . . "Ole Br'er Rabbit, he got de call en he open up lak dis:

" 'Some folks pile up mo'n dey kin tote,
En dat w'at de matter wid King Deer's goat.'

en den Br'er Fox, he make *answer,* 'Dat's so, dat's so, en I'm glad dat it's so.' Den de quills, and de tr'angle, dey come in, en den Br'er Rabbit pursue on wid de call—

" 'Some kill sheep, en some kill shote,
But Br'er Fox kill King Deer goat,'

en den Br'er Fox, he jine in wid de answer, 'I did, I did, en I'm glad dat I did.' "

The writer would add that the story ends with a statement that King Deer came out with his walking cane, and beat the fox, and then invited the rabbit in to eat chicken pie.

From the foregoing one will recognize the naming, by the Negroes themselves, of the parts of their rhymed song, as "call," and "answer." Now just a word concerning the term "answer," instead of "sponse," as used by the writer. You will notice that Mr. Harris records, incidentally, of Br'er Rabbit "dat he sing de *call,* lak de Captain er de co'n pile." This has reference to the singing of the Negroes at corn huskings where the leader sings a kind of solo part, and the others by way of response, sing a kind of chorus. At corn huskings, at plays, and elsewhere, when Negroes sang secular songs, some one was chosen to lead. As a little boy, I witnessed secular singing in all these places. When a leader was chosen, the invariable words of his commission were: "You sing the 'call' and we'll sing the '*sponse.*'" Of course the sentence was not quite so well constructed grammatically, but "call" and "sponse" were the terms always used. This being true, I have felt that I ought to use these terms, though I recognize the probability of there being communities where the word *answer* would be used. All folk terms and writings have different versions.

The "sponses" in most of the Negro Folk Rhymes in our collection are wanting, and the Rhymes themselves, in most cases, consist of calls only. As examples of those with "sponses" left, may be mentioned "Juba" with its sponse "Juba"; "Frog Went A-courting," with its sponse "Uh-huh!"; "Did You Feed My Cow?" with its sponse 'Yes, Ma'am," etc., and "The Old Black Gnats," where the sponses are "I cain't git out'n here, etc."

I shall now endeavor to show why the Negro Folk Rhymes consist in most cases of "calls" only, and how and why the "sponses" have disappeared from the finished product. I record here the notes of two common Negro Play Songs along with sample stanzas used in the singing of them. I hope through a little study of these, to make clear the matter of Folk Rhyme development, to the point of dropping the "sponse."

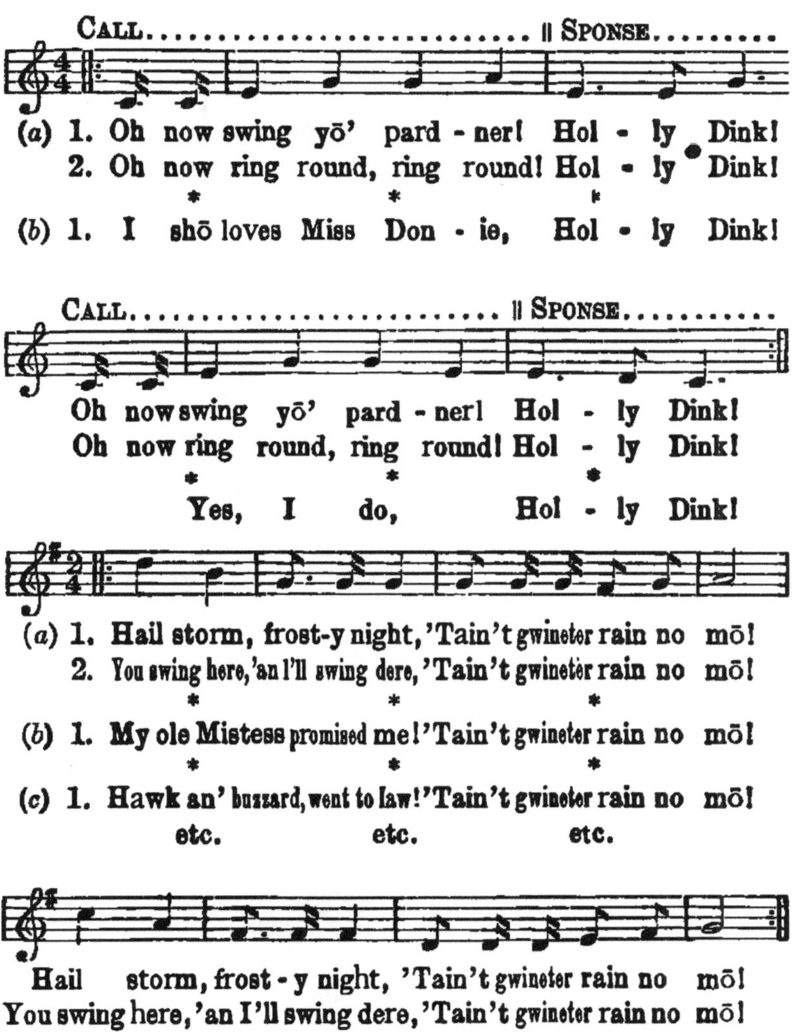
CALL
SPONSE
(a) 1. Oh now swing yō' pard - ner! Hol - ly Dink!
2. Oh now ring round, ring round! Hol - ly Dink!
* * *
(b) 1. I shō loves Miss Don - ie, Hol - ly Dink!
CALL
SPONSE
Oh now swing yō' pard - ner! Hol - ly Dink!
Oh now ring round, ring round! Hol - ly Dink!
* * *
Yes, I do, Hol - ly Dink!
(a) 1. Hail storm, frost-y night, 'Tain't gwineter rain no mō!
2. You swing here, 'an I'll swing dere, 'Tain't gwineter rain no mō!
* * *
(b) 1. My ole Mistess promised me! 'Tain't gwineter rain no mō!
* * *
(c) 1. Hawk an' buzzard, went to law! 'Tain't gwineter rain no mō!
etc. etc. etc.
Hail storm, frost - y night, 'Tain't gwineter rain no mō!
You swing here, 'an I'll swing dere, 'Tain't gwineter rain no mō!
* * *
When she died, she'd set me free, 'Tain't gwineter rain no mō!
* * *
Hawk come back, wid a broken jaw, 'Tain't gwineter rain no mō!
etc. etc. etc.

These simple little songs,—the first made up of five notes, and the second of seven,—are typical Negro Play songs. I shall not describe the simple play which accompanied them because that description would not add to the knowledge of the evolution under consideration.

At a Negro Evening Entertainment several such songs would be sung and played, and some individual would be chosen to lead or sing the "calls" of each of the songs. The 'sponses in some cases were meaningless utterances, like "Holly Dink," given in the first song recorded, while others were made up of some sentence like " 'Tain't Gwineter Rain No Mō'!" found in the second song given. The "sponses" were not expected to bear a special continuous relation in thought to the "calls." Indeed no one ever thought of the 'sponses as conveyers of thought, whether jumbled syllables or sentences. The songs went under the names of the various sponses. Thus the first Play Song recorded was known as "Holly Dink," and the second as " 'Tain't Gwineter Rain No Mō'."

The playing and singing of each of these songs commonly went on continuously for a quarter of an hour or more. This being the case, we scarcely need add that the leader of the Play Song had both his memory and ingenuity taxed to their utmost, in devising enough "calls" to last through so long a period of time of continuous playing and singing. The reader will notice under both of the Play Songs recorded, that I have written under "(a)" two stanzas of prose "calls." I would convey the thought to the reader, by these illustrations, that the one singing the "calls" was at liberty to use, and did use any prose sentence that would fit in with the "call" measures of the song.

Of course these prose "calls" had to be rhythmic to fit into the measures, but much freedom was allowed in respacing the time allotted to notes, and in the redivision of the notes in the "fitting in" process. Even these prose stanzas bore the mark of Rhyme to the Negro fancy. The reader will notice that, where the "call" is in prose, it is always repeated, and thus the line in fancy rhymed with itself. Examples as found in our Second Play Song:

"Hail storm, frosty night.
Hail storm, frosty night."

Now, it was considered by Negroes, in the days gone by, something of an accomplishment for a leader to be able to sing "calls," for so long a time, when they bore some meaning, and still a greater accomplishment to sing the calls both in rhyme and with meaning. This led each individual to rhyme his calls as far as possible because leaders were invited to lead songs during an evening's entertainment, largely in accordance with their ability, and thus those desiring to lead were compelled to make attainment in both rhyme and meaning. Now, the reader will notice under "Holly Dink," heading "(b)," "I shō' loves Miss Donie." This is a part of the opening line of our Negro Rhyme, "Likes and Dislikes." I would convey the thought to the reader that this whole Rhyme, and any other Negro Rhyme which would fit into a 2/4 music measure, could be, and was used by the Play Song leader in singing the calls of "Holly Dink." Thus a leader would lead such a song; and by using one whole Rhyme after another, succeed in rhyming the calls for a quarter of an hour. If his Rhymes "gave out," he used rhythmic prose calls; and since these did not need to have meaning, his store was unlimited. Just as any Rhyme which could be fitted into a 2/4 music measure would be used with "Holly Dink," so any Rhyme which could be fitted into a 4/4 measure would be used with the " 'Tain't Gwineter Rain No Mō'." Illustrations given under "(b)" and "(c)" under the last mentioned song are

—"Promises of Freedom," and "Hawk and Buzzard."

Since all Negro Songs with a few exceptions were written in 4/4 measures and 2/4 measures, and Negro rhymed "calls" were also written in the same way, the rhymed "calls" which may have originated with one song were transferred to, and used with other songs. *Thus the rhymed "calls" becoming detached for use with any and all songs into which they could be fitted, gave rise to the multitude of Negro Folk Rhymes, a small fragment of which multitude is recorded in our collection.* Negro Dances and Dance Rhymes were both constructed in 2/4 and 4/4 measures, and the Rhymes were propagated for that same reason. Rhymes, once detached from their original song or dance, were learned, and often repeated for mere pastime, and thus they were transmitted to others as unit compositions.

We have now seen how detached rhymed "calls" made our Negro Folk Rhymes. Next let us consider how and why whole little "poems" arose in a Play Song. One will notice in reading Negro Folk Rhymes that the larger number of them tell a little story or give some little comic description, or some little striking thought. Since all the Rhymes had to be memorized to insure their continued existence, and since Memory works largely through Association; one readily sees that the putting of the Rhymes into a story, descriptive, or striking thought form, was the only thing that could cause their being kept alive. It was only through their being composed thus that Association was able to assist Memory in recalling them. Those carrying another form carried their death warrant.

Now let us look a little more intimately into how the Rhymes were probably composed. In collecting them, I often had the same Rhyme given to me over and over again by different individuals. Most of the Rhymes were given by different individuals in fragmentary form. In case of all the Rhymes thus received, there would always be a half stanza, or a whole stanza which all contributors' versions held in common. As examples: in "Promises of Freedom," all contributors gave the lines—

"My ole Mistiss promise me
W'en she died, she'd set me free."

In "She Hugged Me and Kissed Me," the second stanza was given by all. In "Old Man Know-All," the first two lines of the last stanza came from all who gave the Rhyme. The writer terms these parts of the individual Rhymes, seemingly known to all who know the "poems," *key verses*. The very fact that the key verses, only, are known to all, seems to me to warrant the conclusion that these were probably the first verses made in each individual Rhyme. Now when an individual made such a key verse, one can easily see that various singers of "calls" using it would attempt to associate other verses of their own making with it in order to remember them all for their long "singing Bees." The story, the description, and the striking thought furnished convenient vehicles for this association of verses, so as to make them easy to keep in memory. This is why the verses of many singers of "Calls" finally became blended into little poem-like Rhymes.

I have pointed out "call" and "sponse," in Rhymes, and have shown how, through them, in song, the form of the Negro Rhyme came into existence. But many of the Pastime Rhymes apparently had no connection with the Play or the Dance. I must now endeavor to account for such Rhymes as these.

In order to do this, I must enter upon the task of trying to show how "call" and "sponse" originated.

The origin of "call" and "sponse" is plainly written on the faces of the rhymes of the Social Instinct type. Read once again the following rhyme recorded in our collection under the caption of "Ante-bellum Courtship Inquiry"—

(He)—"Is you a flyin' lark, or a settin' dove?"
(She)—"I'se a flyin' lark, my Honey Love."
(He)—"Is you a bird o' one fedder, or a bird o' two?"
(She)—I'se a bird o' one fedder, w'en it comes to you."
(He)—"Den Mam:
"I has desire an' quick temptation
To jine my fence to yō' plantation."

This is primitive courtship; direct, quick, conclusive. It is the crude call of one heart, and the crude response of another heart. The two answering and blending into one, in the primitive days, made a rhymed couplet—one. It is "call" and "sponse," born to vibrate in complementary unison with two hearts that beat as one. "Did all Negroes carry on courtship in this manner in olden days?" No, not by any means. Only the more primitive by custom, and otherwise used such forms of courtship. The more intelligent of those who came out of slavery had made the white man's customs their own, and laughed at such crudities, quite as much as we of the present day. The writer thinks his ability to recall from childhood days a clear remembrance of many of these crude things is due to the fact that he belonged to a Negro family that laughed much, early and late, at such things. But the simple forms of "call" and "sponse" were used much in courtship by the more primitive. This points out something of the general origin of "call" and "sponse" in Social Instinct Rhymes, but does not account for their origin in other types of Rhymes. I now turn attention to those.

About eighteen years ago I was making a Sociological investigation for Tuskegee Institute, which carried me into a remote rural district in the Black Belt of Alabama. In the afternoon, when the Negro laborers were going home from the fields and occasionally during the day, these laborers on one plantation would utter loud musical "calls" and the "calls" would be answered by musical responses from the laborers on other plantations. These calls and responses had no peculiar significance. They were only for whatever pleasure these Negroes found in the cries and apparently might be placed in a parallel column alongside of the call of a song bird in the woods being answered by another. Dr. William H. Sheppard, many years a missionary in Congo, Africa, upon inquiry, tells me that similar calls and responses obtain there, though not so musical. He also tells me that the calls have a meaning there. There are calls and responses for those lost in the forest, for fire, for the approach of enemies, etc. These Alabama Negro calls, however, had no meaning, and yet the calls and responses so fitted into each other as to make a little complete tune.

Now, I had heard "field" calls all during my early childhood in Tennessee, and these also were answered by men in adjoining fields. But the Tennessee calls and responses which I remembered had no kinship which would combine them into a kind of little completed song as was the case with the Alabama calls and responses.

Again, in Tennessee when a musical call was uttered by the laborers in one field, those in the other fields around would often use identically the same call as a response. The Alabama calls and responses were short, while those of Tennessee were long.

I am listing an Alabama "call" and "response." I regret that I cannot recall more of them. I am also recording three Tennessee calls or responses (for they may be called either). Then I am recording a fourth one from Tennessee, not exactly a call, but partly call and partly song. The reason for this will appear later. By a study of these I think we can pretty reasonably make a final interesting deduction as to the general origin of "call" and 'sponse" in the form of the types of Rhyme not already discussed.

In the Alabama Field Call and response one cannot help seeing a counterpart in music of the "call" and "sponse" in the words of the types of Rhymes already discussed.

ALABAMA FIELD CALL AND RESPONSE

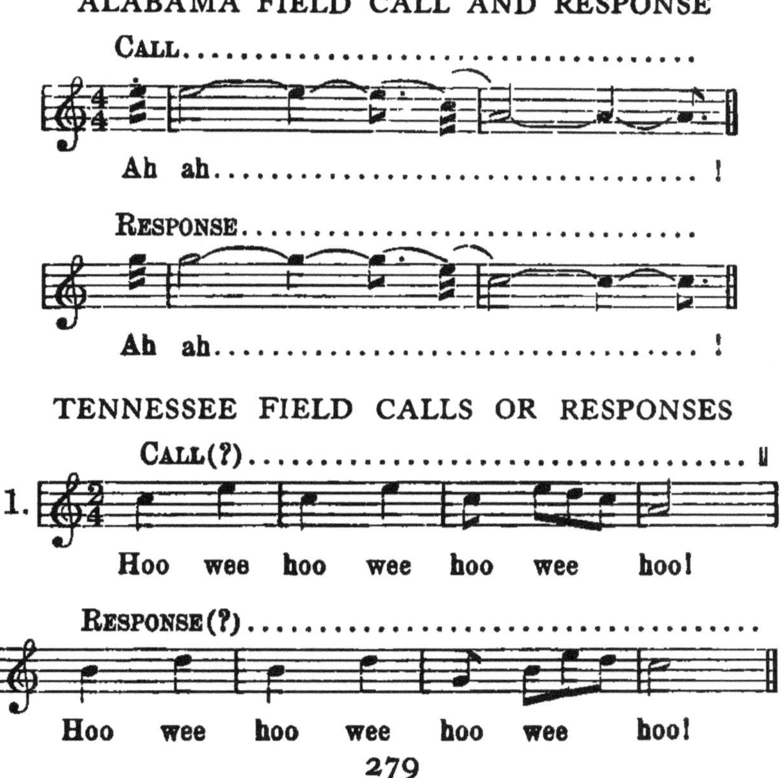

TENNESSEE FIELD CALLS OR RESPONSES

CALL(?)
2
Ah ah.... ah ah..... ah!..........
RESPONSE(?)
Ah ah ah ah... ah.. ah ah ah ah... ah!..
CALL(?)
3.
Ah ah ah ah ah ah ah ah
(Sometimes) I wants a piece a hoecake I wants a piece o' bread.
RESPONSE(?)
Ah ah ah ah...... ah ah..... ah!
Well Ise so tired an' hongry dat Ise almos' dead.
4.
1. Ole Bil - ly Baw - lie "Eh hoo hoo wee!"
2. I hears you hol - ler "Eh hoo hoo wee!"
Ole Bil - ly Baw - lie "Eh hoo wee hoo!"
I hears you hol - ler "Eh hoo wee hoo!"

If one looks at Number 1 under the Tennessee calls or responses, there is nothing to indicate especially that it was ever other than the whole as it is here written. But when he looks at Number 2 under Tennessee calls or responses he is struck with the remarkable fact that it changes right in the midst from the rhythm of the 9/8 measure to that of the 6/8 measure. Now if there be any one characteristic which is constant in Negro music it is that the rhythm remains the same throughout a given production. In a very, very few long Negro productions I have known an occasional change in the time, but *never* in a musical production consisting of a few measures. The only reasonable explanation to be offered for the break in the time of Number 2, as a Negro production, is that it was originally a "call" and "response"; the "call" being in a 9/8 measure and the "response" being in a 6/8 measure. Here then we have "call" and "sponse." It would look as if the Negroes in Tennessee had combined the "calls" and "sponses" into one and had used them as a whole. When we accept this view all the differences, between the Alabama and Tennessee productions, before mentioned are accounted for. Then looking again at Number 1 under Tennessee calls or responses, one sees that it would conveniently divide right in the middle to make a "call" and "sponse." Now look at Number 3 under Tennessee calls. It was usually cried off with the syllable *ah* and would easily divide in the middle. I remember this "call" very distinctly from my childhood because the men giving it placed the thumb upon the larynx and made it vibrate longitudinally while uttering the cry. The thumb thus used produced a peculiar screeching and rattling tone that hardly sounded human. But the words "I want a piece of hoecake, etc.," as recorded under the "call," were often rhymed off in song with it. Thus we trace the form of "call" and "sponse" from the friendly musical greeting between laborers at a distance to the place of the formation of a crude Rhyme to go with it. I would have the reader notice that these words finally supplied were in "call" and "sponse" form. The idea is that one individual says: "I want a piece of hoecake, I want a piece o' bread," and another chimes in by way of response: "Well, I'se so tired and hongry dat I'se almos' dead."

"Ole Billie Bawlie" found as Number 4 was a little song which was used to deride men who had little ability musically to intonate "calls" and "sponses." The name "Bawlie" was applied to emphasize that the individual bawled instead of sounding pleasant notes. It is of interest to us because it is a mixture of Rhyme and Field "call" and completes the connecting links along the line of Evolution between the "call" and "sponse" and the Rhyme.

Wherever one thing is derived from another by process of Evolution, there is the well known biological law that there ought to be every grade of connecting link between the original and the last evolved product. The law holds good here in our Rhymes. If this last statement holds good then the law must be universal. May we be permitted to digress enough to show that the law is universal because, though it is a law whose biological phase has been long recognized, not much attention has been paid to it in other fields.

It holds good in the world of inanimate matter. There are three general classes of chemical compounds: Acids, bases, and salts. But along with these three general classes are found all kinds of connecting links: Acid salts, basic salts, hydroxy acids, etc.

It holds good in the animal and plant worlds. Looking at the ancestors of the horse in geological history we find that the first kind of horse to appear upon the earth was the Œohippus. He had four toes on the hind foot and three on the front one. Through a long period of development, the present day one-toed horse descended from this many-toed primitive horse. There is certainty of the line of descent of the horse because all the connecting links have been discovered in fossil form, between the primitive horse and the present day horse. Plants in like manner show all kinds of connecting links.

The law holds sway in the world of language; and that is the world with which we are concerned here. The state of Louisiana once belonged to the French; now it belongs to an English-speaking people. If one goes among the Creoles in Louisiana he will find a very few who speak almost Parisian French and very poor English. Then he will find a very large number who speak a pure English and a very poor French. Between these classes he will find those speaking all grades of French and English. These last mentioned are the connecting links, and the connecting links bespeak a line of evolution where those of French descent are gradually passing over to a class which will finally speak the English language exclusively.

Now let us turn our attention again directly to the discussion of the evolution of Negro Folk

Rhymes. One can judge whether or not he has discovered the correct line of descent of the Rhymes by seeing whether or not he has all the connecting links requisite to the line of evolution. I think it must be agreed that I have given every type of connecting link between common Field "calls" and "sponses," and incipient crude Negro Rhymes. They set the mold for the other general Negro Rhymes not hitherto discussed.

If the reader will be kind enough to apply the test of connecting links to the Play and other Rhymes already discussed, he will find that the reactions will indicate that we have traced their correct lines of origin and descent.

The spirit of "call" and "sponse" hovers ghostlike over the very thought of many Negro Rhymes. In "Jaybird," the first two lines of each stanza are a call in thought, while the last two lines are a "sponse" in thought to it. The same is true of "He Is My Horse," "Stand Back, Black Man," "Bob-White's Song," "Promises of Freedom," "The Town and the Country Bird," and many others.

Then "call" and "sponse" looms up in the midst in thought between stanza and stanza in many Rhymes. Good examples are found in "The Great Owl's Song," "Sheep and Goat," "The Snail's Reply," "Let's Marry—Courtship," "Shoo! Shoo!" 'When I Go to Marry," and many others.

"Call' and "sponse" even runs, at least in one case, between whole Rhymes. "I Wouldn't Marry a Black Girl" as a "call" has for its "sponse": "I Wouldn't Marry a Yellow or a White Negro Girl." The Rhyme "I'd Rather Be a Negro Than a Poor White Man" is a "sponse" to an imaginary "call" that the Negro is inferior by nature.

After some consideration, as compiler of the Negro Rhymes, I thought I ought to say something of their rhyming system, but before doing this I want to consider for a little the general structure of a stanza in Negro Rhymes.

Of course there is no law, but the number of lines in a stanza of English poetry is commonly a multiple of two. The large majority of Negro Rhymes follows this same rule, but, even in case of these, the lines are so unsymmetrical that they make but the faintest approach to the commonly accepted standards. Then there are Rhymes with stanzas of three lines and there are those with five, six, and seven lines. This is because the imaginary music measure is the unit of measurement instead of feet, and the stanzas are all right so long as they run in consonance with the laws governing music measures and rhythm. In a tune like "Old Hundred" commonly used in churches as a Doxology, there are four divisions in the music corresponding with the four lines of the stanza. Each division is called, in music, a Phrase. Two of these Phrases make a Phrase Group and two Phrase Groups make a Period. Now when one moves musically through a Phrase Group his sense of rhythm is partially satisfied and when he has moved through a Period the sense of Rhythm is entirely satisfied.

When one reads the three line stanzas of Negro Folk Rhymes he passes through a music Period and thus the stanza satisfies in its rhythm. Example:

"Bridle up er rat,
Saddle up er cat,
An' han' me down my big straw hat."

Here the first two lines are a Phrase each and constitute together a Phrase Group. The third line is made up of two Phrases, or a Phrase Group in itself. Thus this third line along with the first two makes a Music Period and the whole satisfies our rhythmic sense though the lines are apparently odd. In all Negro Rhymes, however odd in number and however ragged may seem the lines, the music

Phrases and Periods are there in such symmetry as to satisfy our sense of rhythm.

I now turn attention to the rhyming of the lines in Negro verse. The ordinary systems of rhyming as set forth by our best authors will take in most Negro Rhymes. Most of them are Adjacent and Interwoven Rhymes. There are five systems of rhyming commonly used in the white man's poetry but the Negro Rhyme has nine systems. Here again we find a parallelism, as in case of music scales, etc. Five in each system are the same. The ordinary commonly accepted systems are:

a a	Where the adjacent lines rhyme by twos. We call it "Adjacent rhymes" or a "Couplet."

a b a b	Where the alternating lines rhyme we call it "Alternate" or "Interwoven Rhyme."

a b b a	Where lines 1 and 4, and 2 and 3 rhyme respectively with each other. This is called "Close Rhyme."

a
b
c
b — Where in a stanza of four lines, lines 2 and 4 only rhyme. This is sometimes also called "Alternate Rhyme."

a
a
b
a — Where in a stanza of four lines 1, 2 and 4 rhyme. This is called "Interrupted Rhyme."

I now beg to offer a system of classification in rhyming which will include all Negro Rhymes. I shall insert the ordinary names in parenthesis along with the new names wherever the system coincides with the ordinary system for white men's Rhymes. The only reason for not using the old names exclusively in these places is that nomenclature should be kept consistent in any proposed classification, so far as that is possible.

In classifying the rhyming of the lines or verses I have borrowed terms from the gem world, partly because the Negro hails from Africa, a land of gems; and partly because the verses bear whatever beauty there might have been in his crude crystalized thoughts in the dark days of his enslavement.

I present herewith the outline and follow it with explanations:

Class	*Systems*
I Rhythmic Solitaire.	(a) Rhythmic measured lines
II Rhymed Doublet	(a) Regular (Adjacent Rhyme) (b) Divided (Includes Close Rhyme) (c) Supplemented.
III Rhyming Doublet	(a) Regular (Includes Alternate Rhyme) (b) Inverted (Close Rhyme)
IV Rhymed Cluster	(a) Regular (b) Divided (Interrupted Rhyme) (c) Supplemented

I a Rhythmic Solitaire, Rhythmic measured lines. In many Rhymes there is a rhythmic line dropped in here and there that doesn't rhyme with any other line. They are rhythmic like the other lines and serve equally to fill out the music Phrases and Periods. These are the Rhythmic Solitaires and because of their solitaire nature it follows that there is only one system. Examples are found in the first line of each stanza of "Likes and Dislikes"; in the second line of each stanza of "Old Aunt Kate;" in lines five and six of each stanza of "I'll Wear Me a Cotton Dress," in lines three and four of the "Sweet Pinks Kissing Song," etc. The Rhythmic Solitaires do not seem to have been largely used by Negroes for whole compositions. Only one whole Rhyme in our collection is written with Rhythmic Solitaires. That Rhyme is: "Song to the Runaway Slave." This Rhyme is made up of blank verse as measured by the white man's standard.

II a. The Regular Rhymed Doublet. This is the same as our common Adjacent Rhyme. There are large numbers of Negro Rhymes which belong to this system. The "Jaybird" is a good example.

II b. The Divided Rhymed Doublet. It includes Close Rhyme and there are many of this system. In ordinary Close Rhyme one set of rhyming lines (two in number) is separated by two intervening lines, but this "Rhyming Couplet" in Negro Rhymes may be separated by three lines as in "Bought Me a Wife," where the divided doublet consists of lines 3 and 7. Then the Divided Rhymed Doublet may be separated by only one line, as in "Good-by, Wife," where the Doublet is found in lines 5 and 7.

II c. The Supplemented Rhymed Doublet. It is illustrated by "Juba" found in our collection. The words "Juba! Juba!" found following the second line of each stanza, are the supplement. I shall take up the explanation of Supplemented Rhyme later, since the explanation goes with all Supplemented Rhyme and not with the Doublet only. I consider the Supplement one of the things peculiarly characteristic of Negro Rhyme. The following stanza illustrates such a Supplemented Doublet:

"Juba jump! Juba sing!
Juba cut dat Pidgeon's Wing! Juba! Juba"

Representing such a rhyming by letters we have

(a
(a - x

III. The Rhyming Doublet. It is generally made up of two consecutive lines not rhyming with each other but so constructed that one of the lines will rhyme with one line of another Doublet similarly constructed and found in the same stanza.

III a. The Regular Rhyming Doublet. It is the same as our common interwoven rhyme and is very common among Negro Rhymes. There is one peculiar Interwoven Rhyme found in our collection; it is "Watermelon Preferred." In it the second Rhyming Doublet is divided by a kind of parenthetic Rhythmic Solitaire.

III b. The Inverted Rhyming Doublet. It is the same as our ordinary Close Rhyme.

The writer had expected to find the Supplemented Rhyming Doublet among Negro Rhymes but peculiarly enough it does not seem to exist.

IV a. The Regular Rhymed Cluster. It consists of three consecutive lines in the same stanza which rhyme. An example is found in "Bridle Up a Rat," one of whose stanzas we have already quoted. It is represented by the lettering (a
(a
(a

IV. b. The Divided Rhymed Cluster. It includes ordinary Interrupted Rhyme—with the lettering (a An example is found in the Ebo or
(a Guinea Rhyme "Tree Frogs."
(b
(a

But in Negro Folk Rhymes two lines may divide the

Rhymed Cluster instead of one. An example of this is found in "Animal Fair," whose rhyming may be represented by the lettering

(a
(a
(b
(b
(a

IV c. The Supplemented Rhymed Clusters. They are well represented in Negro Rhymes. Some have a single supplement as in "Negroes Never Die," whose rhyming is lettered

(a
(a
(a - x

Some have double supplements as in "Frog Went a-Courting" whose rhyming is lettered

(a - x
(a
(a - x

Now Negroes did not retain, permanently, meaningless words in their Rhymes. The Rhymes themselves were "calls" and had meaning. The "sponses," such as "Holly Dink," "Jing-Jang," "Oh, fare you well," " 'Tain't gwineter rain no more," etc., that had no meaning, died year after year and new "sponses" and songs came into existence.

Let us see what these permanently retained seemingly senseless Supplements mean.

In "Frog Went a-Courting" we see the Supplement "uh-huh! uh-huh!" It is placed in the midst to keep vividly before the mind of the listener the ardent singing of the frog in Spring during his courtship season, while we hear a recounting of his adventures. It is to this Simple Rhyme what stage scenery is to the Shakespearian play or the Wagnerian opera. It seems to me (however crude his verse) that the Negro has here suggested something new to the field of poetry. He suggests that, while one recounts a story or what not, he could to advantage use words at the same time having no bearing on the story to depict the surroundings or settings of the production. The gifted Negro poet, Paul Laurence Dunbar, has used the supplement in this way in one of his poems. The poem is called "A Negro Love Song." The little sentence, "Jump back, Honey, jump back," is thrown in, in the midst and at the end of each stanza. Explaining it, the following is written by a friend, at the heading of this poem:

"During the World's Fair he (Mr. Dunbar) served for a short time as a hotel waiter. When the Negroes were not busy they had a custom of congregating and talking about their sweethearts. Then a man with a tray would come along and, as the dining-room was frequently crowded, he would say when in need of passing room, 'Jump back, Honey, jump back.' Out of the commonplace confidences, he wove the musical little composition—'A Negro Love Song.' "

Now, this line, "Jump back, Honey, jump back," was used by Mr. Dunbar to recall and picture before the mind the scurrying hotel waiter as he bragged to his fellows of his sweetheart and told his tales of adventure. It is the "stage scenery" method used by the slave Negro verse maker. Mr. Dunbar uses this style also in "A Lullaby," "Discovered," "Lil' Gal" and "A Plea." Whether he used it knowingly in all cases, or whether he instinctively sang in the measured strains of his benighted ancestors, I do not know.

The Supplement was used in another way in Negro Folk Dance Rhymes. I have already explained how the Rhymes were used in a general way in the Dance. Let us glance at the Dance Rhyme "Juba" with its Supplement, "Juba! Juba!" to illustrate this special use of the Supplement. "Juba" itself was a kind of dance step. Now let us imagine two dancers in a circle of men to be dancing while the following lines are being patted and repeated:

"Juba Circle, raise de latch,
Juba dance dat Long Dog Scratch, Juba! Juba!"

While this was being patted and repeated, the dancers within the circle described a circle with raised foot and ended doing a dance step called "Dog Scratch." Then when the Supplement "Juba! Juba!" was said the whole circle of men joined in the dance step "Juba" for a few moments. Then the next stanza would be repeated and patted with the same general order of procedure.

The Supplement, then, in the Dance Rhyme was used as the signal for all to join in the dance for a while at intervals after they had witnessed the finished foot movements of their most skilled dancers.

The Supplement was used in a third way in Negro Rhymes. This is illustrated by the Rhyme, "Anchor Line" where the Supplement is "Dinah." This was a Play Song and was commonly used as such, but the Negro boy often sang such a song to his sweetheart, the Negro father to his child, etc. When such songs were sung on other occasions than the Play, the name of the person to whom it was being sung was often substituted for the name Dinah. Thus it would be sung

"I'se gwine out on de Anchor Line—Mary," etc.

The Supplement then seems to have been used in some cases to broaden the scope of direct application of the Rhyme.

The last use of the Supplement to be mentioned is closely related in its nature to the "stage scenery" use already mentioned. This kind of Supplement is used to depict the mental condition or attitude of an individual passing through the experiences being related. Good examples are found in "My First and My Second Wife" where we have the Supplements, "Now wusn't I sorrowful in mind," etc.; and in "Stinky Slave Owners" with its Supplements "Eh-Eh!" "Sho-shȯ!" etc.

The Negro Rhymes here and there also have some kind of little introductory word or line to each stanza. I consider this also something peculiar to Negro Rhyme. I have named these little introductory words or sentences the "Verse Crown." They are receivers into which verses are set and serve as dividing lines in the production. As the reader knows, the portion of the ring which receives the gems and sets them into a harmonious whole is called the "Crown." Having borrowed the terms Solitaire, Doublet, etc., for the verses, the name for these introductory words and lines automatically became "Verse Crown."

Just as I have figuratively termed the Supplements in one place "stage scenery," so I may with equal propriety term the "Verse Crown" the "rise" or the "fall" of the stage curtain. They separate the little Acts of the Rhymes into scenes. As an example read the comic little Rhyme "I Walked the Roads." The word "Well" to the first stanza marks the raising of the curtain and we see the ardent Negro boy lover nonsensically prattling to the one of his fancy about everything in creation until he is so tired that he can scarcely stand erect. The curtain drops and rises with the word "Den.' In this, the second scene, he finally gets around to the point where he makes all manner of awkward protestations of love. The hearer of the Rhyme is left laughing, with a sort of satisfactory feeling that possibly he succeeded in his suit and possibly he didn't. Among the many examples of Rhymes where verse crowns serve as curtains to divide the Acts into scenes may be mentioned "I Wish I Was an Apple," "Rejected by Eliza Jane," "Courtship," "Plaster," "The Newly Weds," and "Four Runaway Negroes."

Though the stanzas in Negro Rhymes commonly have just one kind of rhyming, in some cases as many as three of the systems of rhyming are found in one stanza. I venture to suggest the calling of those with one system "Simple Rhymed Stanzas;" those with two, "Complex Rhymed Stanzas;" those with more than two "Complicated Complex Rhymed Stanzas."

I next call attention to the seeming parodies found occasionally among Negro Rhymes. The words of most Negro parodies are such that they are not fit for print. We have recorded three: "He Paid Me Seven," Parody on "Now I Lay Me Down to Sleep," and Parody on "Reign, Master Jesus, Reign." We can best explain the nature of the Negro Parody by taking that beautiful and touching well-known Jubilee song, "Steal Away to Jesus" and briefly recounting the story of its origin. Its history is well known. We hope the reader will not be disappointed when we say that this song is a parody in the sense in which Negroes composed and used parodies.

The words around which the whole song ranges itself are "Steal away to Jesus, I hain't got long to stay here." Now the slave Negroes on the far away plantations of the South occasionally met in the dead of night in some secluded lonely spot for a religious meeting even when they had been forbidden to do so by their masters. So they made up this song,

"Steal away to Jesus, I hain't got long to stay here." Late in the afternoons when the slaves on any plantation sang it, it served as a notice to slaves on other plantations that a secret religious meeting was to be held that night at the place formerly mutually agreed upon for meetings.

Now here is where the parody comes in under the Negro standard: To the slave master the words meant that his good, obedient slaves were only studying how to be good and to get along peaceably, because they considered, after all, that their time upon earth was short and not of much consequence; but to the listening Negro it meant both a notification of a meeting and slaves disobedient enough to go where they wanted to go. To the listening master it meant that the Negro was thinking of what a short time it would be before he would die and leave the earth, but to the listening slaves it meant that he was thinking of how short a time it would be before he left the cotton field for a pleasant religious meeting. All these meanings were truly literally present but the meaning apparent depended upon the viewpoint of the listener. It was composed thus, so that if the master suspected the viewpoint of the slave hearers, the other viewpoint, intended for him, might be held out in strong relief.

Now let us consider the parodies recorded in our Collection. The Parody on the beautiful little child prayer, "Now I lay me down to sleep" is but the bitter protest from the heart of the woman who, after putting the little white children piously repeating this child prayer, "Now I lay me down to sleep," in their immaculate beds, herself retired to a vermin infested cabin with no time left for cleaning it. It was a tirade against the oppressor but the comic, good-natured "It means nothing" was there to be held up to those calling the one repeating it to task. The parody on "Reign, Master Jesus, Reign!" when heard by the Master meant only a good natured jocular appeal to him for plenty of meat and bread, but with the Negro it was a scathing indictment of a Christian earthly master who muzzled those who produced the food. "He Paid Me Seven" is a mock at the white man for failing to practice his own religion but the clown mask is there to be held up for safety to any who may see the *real* side and take offense.

Slave parodies, then, are little Rhymes capable of two distinct interpretations, both of which are true. They were so composed that if a slave were accused through one interpretation, he could and would truthfully point out the other meaning to the accuser and thus escape serious trouble.

Under all the classes of Negro Rhymes, with the exception of the one Marriage Ceremony Rhyme, there were those which were sung and played on instruments. Since instrumental music called into existence some of the very best among Negro Rhymes it seems as if a little ought to be said concerning the Negro's instruments. Banjos and fiddles (violins) were owned only limitedly by antebellum Negroes. Those who owned them mastered them to such a degree that the memory of their skill will long linger, These instruments are familiar and need no discussion.

Probably the Negro's most primitive instrument, which he could call his very own, was "Quills." It is mentioned in the story, "Brother Fox, Brother Rabbit, and King Deer's Daughter" which I have already quoted at some length. If the reader will notice in this story he will see, after the singing of the first stanza by the rabbit and fox, a description in these words, "Den de quills and de tr'angle, dey come in, an' den Br'er Rabbit pursue on wid de call." Here we have described in the Negro's own way the long form of instrumental music composition which we have hitherto discussed, and "quills" and "tr'angles" are given as the instruments.

In my early childhood I saw many sets of "Quills." They were short reed pipes, closed at one end, made from cane found in our Southern canebrakes. The reed pipes were made closed at one end by being so cut that the bottom of each was a node of the cane. These pipes were "whittled" square with a jack knife and were then wedged into a wooden frame, and the player blew them with his mouth. The "quills," or reed pipes, were cut of such graduated lengths that they constituted the Negro's peculiar music Scale. The music intervals though approximating those of the Caucasian scale were not the same. At times, when in a reminiscent humor, I hum to myself some little songs of my childhood. On occasions, afterwards, I have "picked out" some of the same tunes on the piano. When I have done this I have always felt like giving its production on the piano the same greeting that I gave a friend who had once worn a full beard but had shaved. My greeting was "Hello, friend A; I came near not knowing you."

"Quills" were made in two sets. They were known as a "Little Set of Quills" and a "Big Set of Quills." There were five reeds in the Little Set but I do not know how many there were in a Big Set. I think there were more than twice as many as in a Little Set. I have inserted a cut of a Little Set of "Quills." (Figure I.) The fact that I was in the class of "The Little Boy Who Couldn't Count Seven" when I saw and handled quills makes it necessary to explain how it comes that I am sure of the number of "Quills" in a "Little Set." I recall the intricate tune that could be played only by

A LITTLE SET OF QUILLS

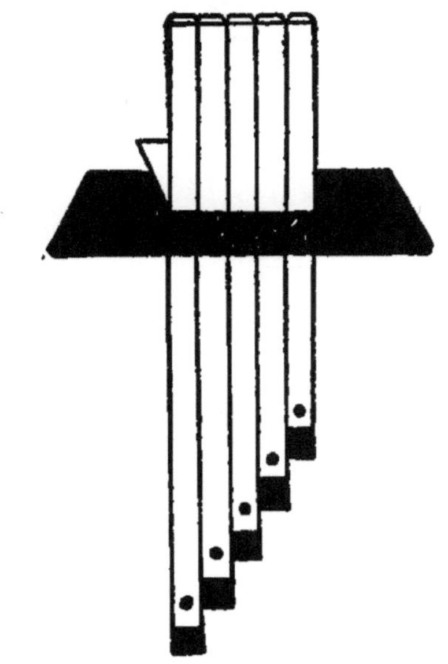

FIGURE I

the performer's putting in the lowest pitched note with his voice. I am herewith presenting that tune, and "blocking out" the voice note there are only five notes left, thus I know there were five "Quills" in the set. I thought a tune played on a "Big Set" might be of interest and so I am giving one of those also. If there be those who would laugh at the crudity of "Quills" it might not be amiss to remember in justice to the inventors that "Quills" constitute a pipe organ in its most rudimentary form.

TUNE PLAYED ON A LITTLE SET OF QUILLS

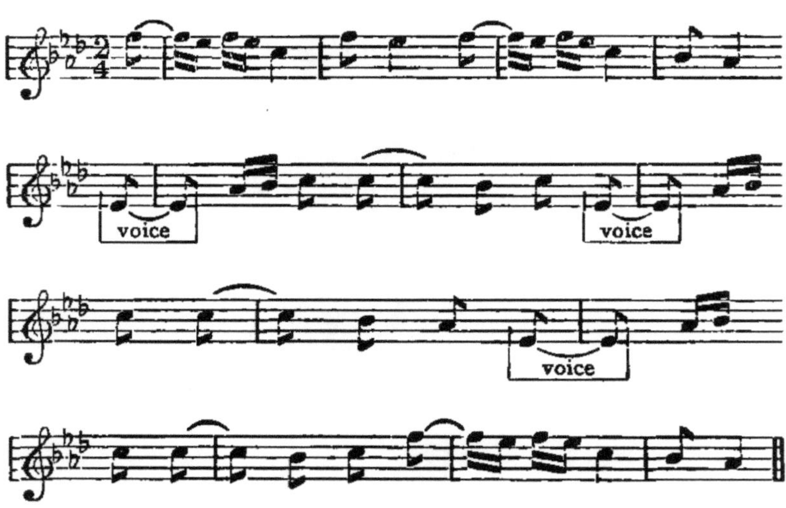

TUNE PLAYED ON A BIG SET OF QUILLS

The "tr'angle" or triangle mentioned as the other primitive instrument used by the rabbit and fox in serenading King Deer's family was only the U-shaped iron clives which with its pin was used for hitching horses to a plow. The ante-bellum Negro often suspended this U-shaped clives by a string and beat it with its pin along with the playing on 'Quills" much after the order that a drum is beaten. These crude instruments produced music not of unpleasant strain and inspired the production of some of the best Negro Rhymes.

I would next consider for a little the origin of the subject matter found in Negro Rhymes. When the Negro sings "Master Is Six Feet One Way" or "The Alabama Way" there is no question where the subject matter came from. But when he sings of animals, calling them all "Brother" or "Sister," and "Bought Me a Wife," etc., the origin of the conception and subject matter is not so clear. I now come to the question: From whence came such subject matter?

First of all, Mr. Joel Chandler Harris, in his introduction to "Nights with Uncle Remus," has shown that the Negro stories of our country have counterparts in the Kaffir Tales of Africa. He therefore leaves strong grounds for inference that the American Negroes probably brought the dim outlines of their Br'er Rabbit stories along with them when they came from Africa. I have already pointed out that some of the Folk Rhymes belong to these Br'er Rabbit stories. Since the origin of the subject matter of one is the origin of the subject matter of the other, it follows that we are reasonably sure of the origin of such Folk Rhymes because of the "counterpart" data presented by Mr. Harris.

But I have been fortunate enough recently to secure direct evidence that one of the American Negro stories recorded by Mr. Harris came from Africa.

While collecting our Rhymes, I asked Dr. C. C. Fuller of the South African Mission, at Chikore, Melsetter, Rhodesia, Africa, for an African Rhyme in Chindau. I might add parenthetically: I have never seen pictures of a cruder or more primitive people than these people who speak Chindau. He obtained and sent me the Rhyme "The Turkey Buzzard" found in our Foreign Section. It was given to him by the Reverend J. E. Hatch of the South African General Mission. Along with this rhyme came the following in his kind and obliging letter: "We thought the story of how the Crocodile got its scaly skin might be of interest also":

"Why the Crocodile Has a Hard, Scaly Skin."

"Long ago the Crocodile had a soft skin like that of the other animals. He used to go far from the rivers and catch animals and children and by so doing annoyed the people very much. So one day when he was far away from water, they surrounded him and set the grass on fire on every side, so that he could not escape to the river without passing through the fire. The fire overtook him and scorched and seared his back, so that from that day his skin has been hard and scaly, and he no longer goes far from the rivers."

This is about as literal an outline of the American Negro story "Why the Alligator's Back is Rough" as one could have. The slight difference is that the direct African version mixes people in with the plot. This along with Mr. Harris's evidences practically establishes the fact that the Negro animal story outlines came with the Negroes themselves from Africa and would also render it practically certain that many animal rhymes came in the same way since these Rhymes in many cases accompany the stories.

Then there are Rhymes, not animal Rhymes, which seem to carry plainly in their thought content a probable African origin. In the Rhyme, "Bought Me a Wife," there is not only the mentioning of buying a wife, but there is the setting forth of feeding her along with guineas, chickens, etc., out under a tree. Such a conception does not fit in with American slave life but does fit into widely prevailing conditions found in Africa.

Read the last stanza of "Ration Day," where the slave sings of going after death to a land where there are trees that bear fritters and where there are ponds of honey. Surely there is nothing in America to suggest such thoughts, but such thoughts might have come from Africa where natives gather their fruit from the bread tree and dip it into honey gathered from the forests.

Read "When My Wife Dies." This is a Dance Rhyme Song. When the Rhymer chants in seemingly light vein in our hearing that he will simply get another wife when his wife dies, we turn away our faces in disgust, but we turn back almost amazed when he announces in the immediately succeeding lines that his heart will sorrow when she is gone because none better has been created among women. The dance goes on and we almost see grim Death himself smile as the Rhymer closes his Dance Song with directions not to bury him deep, and to put bread in his hand and molasses at his feet that he may eat on the way to the "Promised Land."

If you had asked a Negro boy in the days gone by what this Dance Rhyme Song meant, he would have told you that he didn't know, that it was simply an old song he had picked up from somewhere. Thus he would go right along thoughtlessly singing or repeating and passing the Rhyme to others. The dancing over the dead and the song which accompanied it certainly had no place in American life. But do you ask where there was such a place? Get Dr.

William H. Sheppard's "Presbyterian Pioneers in Congo" and read on page 136 the author's description of the behavior of the Africans in Lukenga's Land on the day following the death of one of their fellow tribesmen. It reads in part as follows: "The next day friends from neighboring villages joined with these and in their best clothes danced all day. These dances are to cheer up the bereaved family and to run away evil spirits." Dr. Sheppard also tells us that in one of the tribes in Africa where he labored, a kind of funnel was pushed down into the grave and down this funnel food was dropped for the deceased to feed upon. I have heard from other missionaries to other parts of Africa similar accounts. The minute you suppose the Rhyme "When My Wife Dies" to have had its origin in Africa, the whole thought content is explained. Of course the stanza concerning the pickling of the bones in alcohol is probably of American origin but I doubt not that the thought of the "key verses" came from Africa.

These Rhymes whose thought content I have just discussed I consider only illustrative of the many Rhymes whose thought drift came from Africa.

Many of the Folk Rhymes fall under the heading commonly denominated "Nature Rhymes." By actual count more than a hundred and fifty recorded by the writer have something in their stanzas concerning some animal. I do not think the makers of these Rhymes were makers of Nature Rhymes in the ordinary sense of the term. It would really be more to the point to call them "Animal Rhymes" instead of "Nature Rhymes." With the exception of about a half dozen Rhymes which mention some kind of tree or plant, all the other Rhymes with Nature allusions pertain to animals. The Uncle Remus stories recorded by Joel Chandler Harris are practically all animal stories. I have said in my foregoing discussion that the Negro communed with Nature and she gave him Rhymes for amusement. This is true, but when we say "communed" we simply express a vague intangible something the existence of which lives somewhere in a kind of mental fiction.

Though I was brought up with the Rhymes I make no pretensions that I really know why so many of them were made concerning the animal world. I have heard no Negro tradition on this point. I have thought much on it and I now beg the reader to walk with me over the peculiar paths along which my mind has swept in its search for the truth of this mystery of Animal Rhyme.

Before the great American Civil War the Negro

slave preachers could not, as a class, read and they were taught their Bible texts by white men, commonly their owners. The texts taught them embraced most of the central truths of our Bible. The subjects upon which the ante-bellum Negro preached, however, were comparatively few. Of course a very few ante-bellum Negro preachers could read. In case of these individuals their texts and subjects were scarcely limited by the "lids" of the Bible. I heard scores of these men preach in my childhood days.

The following subjects embrace about all those known to the average of these slave preachers. 1. Joshua. 2. Samson. 3. The Ark. 4. Jacob. 5. Pharaoh and Moses. 6. Daniel. 7. Ezekiel—vision of the valley of dry bones. 8. Judgment Day. 9. Paul and Silas in jail. 10. Peter. 11. John's vision on the Isle of Patmos. 12. Jesus Christ—his love and his miracles. 13. "Servants, obey your Masters."

Now it is strange enough that the ignorant slave, while adopting his Master's religious topics, refused to adopt his hymns and proceeded to make his own songs and to cluster all these songs in thought around the Bible subjects with which he was acquainted. If the reader will get nearly any copy of Jubilee Songs he will find that the larger number group themselves about Jesus Christ and the others cluster about Moses, Daniel, Judgment Day, etc., subjects partially known and handled by the preachers in their sermons. There is just one exception. There is no Jubilee Song on "Servants, obey your Masters." We shall leave for the "feeble" imagination of the reader the reason why. The Negroes practically left out of their Jubilee Songs, Jeremiah, Job, Abraham, Isaac, Solomon, Samuel, Ezra, Mark, Luke, John, James, The Psalms, The Proverbs, etc., simply because these subjects did not fall among those taught them as preaching subjects.

Now let us consider for a while the Negro's religion in Africa. Turning to Bettanny's "The World's Religions" we learn the following facts about aboriginal African worship.

The Bushmen worshiped a Caddis worm and an antelope (a species of deer). The Damaras believed that they and all living creatures descended from a kind of tree and they worshiped that tree. The Mulungu worshiped alligators and lion-shaped idols. The Fantis considered snakes and many other animals messengers of spirits. The Dahomans worshiped snakes, a silk tree, a poison tree and a kind of ocean god whom they called Hu.

Now turning our attention to Negro Folk

Rhymes we find them clustering around the animals f aboriginal African Folk worship. The Negro tories recorded by Mr. Harris center around these nimals also. In the Folk Rhyme "Walk Tom Wilon" our hero steps on an alligator. In "The Ark" he lion almost breaks out of his enclosure of palings. n one rhyme the snake is described as descended rom the Devil and then the Devil figures promiiently in many Rhymes. Then we have "Green Dak Tree Rocky-o" answering to the tree worship.

I have placed in our collection of Rhymes a small oreign section including African Rhymes. I have ecorded precious few but those few are enough o show two things. (1) That the Negro of savage Africa has the rhyme-making habit and probably ias always had it, and thus the American Negro rought this habit with him to America. (2) That ı small handful from darkest Africa contains stanzas on the owl, the frog, and the turkey buzzard just like the American rhymes.

Knowing that the Negro made rhymes in Africa, ind knowing that he centered his Jubilee Song vords around his American Christian religion, is it iot reasonable to suppose that he centered his secılar or African Rhymes around his African reigion? He must have done so unless he changed all his rhyme-making habits after coming to America, for he certainly clustered his American verse largely around his religion. Assuming this to be true the large amount of animal lore in Negro rhyme and story is at once explained.

Possibly the greatest hindrance to one's coming to this conclusion is the fact that the Rabbit and some other animals found in Negro rhyme and story do not appear in the records among those worshiped by aboriginal Africans. The known record of the Africans' early religion covers only a very few pages. Christians have not been willing to spend any time to speak of in investigating the religions of the primitive and the lowly. Thus if these animals were widely worshiped it would not be strange if we should never have heard of it. Let us consider what is known, however.

Taking up the matter of the rabbit Mr. John McBride, Jr., had a very fine and lengthy discussion on "Br'er Rabbit in the Folk Tales of the Negro and other Races" in *The Sewanee Review,* April, 1911. On page 201 of that journal's issue we find these words: "Among the Hottentots, for example, there is a story in which the hare appears in the moon and of which several versions are extant. The story goes that the moon sent the hare to the earth to inform men that, as she died away and rose again, so should all men die and again come to life," etc. I drop the story here because so much of it suffices my purpose. It brings out the fact that the African here had probably truly considered the Rabbit as a messenger of the moon. Now the fact that the Hottentots were thus talking in lore of receiving messages concerning immortality from the moon means there must have been at least a time in their history when they considered the Moon a kind of super-being, a kind of god.

I quote again from Dr. Sheppard's "Presbyterian Pioneers in Congo," page 113. "King Lukenga offers up a sacrifice of a goat or lamb on every new moon. The blood is sprinkled on a large idol in his own fetich house, in the presence of all his counselors. This sacrifice is for the healthfulness of all the King's country, for the crops," etc.

I think after considering the foregoing one will see that there are those of Africa who connect their worship with the moon. We learn also that there are those who claim the rabbit to be the moon's messenger. From this, if we should accept the theory for Animal Rhymes advanced, we would easily see why the rabbit as a messenger of a god or gods would figure so largely in Rhyme and in story. We also would easily see how and why as a messenger of a god he would become "Brother Rabbit." If one will read the little Rhyme "Jaybird" he will notice that the rhymer places the intelligence of the rabbit above his own. Our theory accounts for this.

I would next consider the frog, but I imagine I hear the reader saying: "That is not a beginning. How about your bear, terrapin, wolf, squirrel, etc.?"

Seeing that I am faced by so large an array of animals, I beg the reader to walk with me through just one more little path of thought and with his consent I shall leave the matter there.

We see, in two of our African Rhymes, lines on a buzzard and an owl; yet these African natives do not worship these birds. The American Negro children of my childhood repeated Folk Rhymes concerning the rabbit, the fox, etc., without any thought whatever of worshiping them. These American children had received the whole through dim traditional rhymes and stories and engaged in passing them on to others without any special thought. The uncivilized and the unlettered hand down everything by word of mouth. Religion, trades, superstition, medicine, sense, and nonsense all flow in the same stream and from this stream all is drunk down without question. If therefore the Negro's rhyme-clustering habit in America was the same as it had ever been and the centering of rhymes about animals is due to a former worship of them in Africa, the verses would include not only the animals worshiped in modern Africa but in ancient Africa. The verses would take in animals included in any accepted African religion antedating the comparatively recent religions found there.

The Bakuba tribe have a tradition of their origin. Quoting from Dr. Sheppard's book again, page 114, we have the following: "From all the information I can gather, they (the Bakuba) migrated from the far North, crossed rivers and settled on the high table land." Here is one tradition, standing as a guide post, with its hand pointing toward Egypt. A one fact premise practically never forms a safe basis for a conclusion, but when we couple this tradition with the fact that, so far as we know, men originated in Southwest Asia and therefore probably came into Africa by way of the Isthmus of Suez, I think the case of the Bakuba hand pointing toward a near Egyptian residence a strong one. Now turn to your Encyclopedia Britannica, Vol. X, ninth edition, with American revisions and additions, to the article on "Glass," page 647. Near the bottom of the second column on that page we read: "The

Phoenicians probably derived this knowledge of the art (of glass making) from Egypt. * * * It seems probable that the earliest products of the industry of Phoenicia in the art of glass making are the colored beads which have been found in almost all parts of Europe, in India, and other parts of Asia, and in *Africa.* The "aggry" beads so much valued by the *Ashantees and other natives* of that part of Africa which lies near the Gold Coast, have *probably* the same origin. * * * Their wide dispersion may be referred with much probability to their having been objects of barter between the Phoenician merchants and the barbarous inhabitants of the various countries with which they traded." Here are evidences, then, that the African in his prehistoric days traded with somebody who bartered in beads of Phoenician or Egyptian make. I say Egyptian or Phoenician because if the Phoenicians got this art from the Egyptians I think it would be very difficult for those who lived thousands of years afterward to be sure in which country a specific bead was made, the art as practiced by one country being a kind of copy of the art as practiced in the other country. With the historic record that the Phoenicians were the great traders of the Ancient World our writers attributed the carrying of the beads into Africa, among the natives, to the Phoenicians. Without questioning these time-honored conclusions, we do know that Egyptian caravans still make journeys into the interior of Africa for the purpose of trade. Shall we think this trading practice on the part of Egypt in Africa one of recent origin or probably one that runs back through the centuries? I see no reason for believing this trading custom to be other than an ancient one. If the ancient Egyptians traded with the surrounding Africans and these Africans gradually migrated South, as is stated in the Bakuba tradition, the whole matter of how all kinds of animals got mixed into Negro Folk Rhymes by custom becomes clear. It also will explain how animal worship got scattered throughout Africa, for it is the unbroken history of the world that traders of a race superior in attainment always somehow manage to carry along their religion to the race inferior in attainment. The religious emissaries generally follow along in the wake of the traders. If we make the assumption, on the foregoing grounds, that the very ancient African Negro got in touch with the religion of Ancient Egypt, then the appearance of the frog, birds, etc., in Negro Rhyme is explained, for if we read the lists of animal gods of Ancient Egypt and the animal states through which spirits were supposed to pass, we have no trouble finding the list of animals extolled in Negro rhyme and story.

If Negro Rhyme has always centered about Negro religion, then when the Negro was brought to America and began changing his religion, he should have had some songs or rhymes on the dividing line between the old and the new. In other words, there ought to be connecting links between "secular" Folk Rhymes and Jubilee Songs, songs that by nature partake of both types. This must happen in order to be in accord with the law of the presence of connecting links where evolution produces a new type from an old one. By using the procedure under Mendel's law of mating like descendants from a cross between two and by eliminating those who do not reproduce constant to the type which we are trying to produce, we can produce a new and constant type in the third succeeding generation of descendants.

Now the Negro slave turned quickly in America from heathenism to Christianity. This was accomplished through white Christians correcting and eliminating all thoughts and productions which hovered on the border line between heathen ideals and Christianity. They used the Mendelian procedure of eliminating all crosses that did not give a product with Christian characteristics and thus necessarily eliminated Rhymes or songs of the connecting link type. They did a good thorough job but the writer believes he sees two connecting links that escaped their sensitive ears and sharp eyes. They are Jubilee songs; one is "Keep inching along like a poor inch worm, Jesus will come by-and-by," the other is "Go chain the lion down before the Heaven doors close."

The reader will recall that I have already shown that the worm and the lion were connected with native African worship. Of course we all know quite well that a "Caddis worm" is not an "Inch worm," but for a man trying to turn from the old to the new, from idolatry to Christianity, a closer relation than this might not be very comfortable neutral ground.

The following Folk Rhymes found in our collection might also pass for connecting links: "Jawbone," "Outrunning the Devil," "How to Get to Glory Land," "The Ark," "Destinies of Good and Bad Children," "How to Keep or Kill the Devil," "Ration Day," and "When My Wife Dies." The superstitions of the Negro Rhymes are possibly only fossils left in one way or another by ancient native African worship.

In a few Rhymes the vice of stealing is either

laughed at, or apparently laughed at. Such Rhymes carry on their face a strictly American slave origin. An example is found in "Christmas Turkey." If one asks how I know its origin to be American, the answer is that the native African had no such thing as Christmas and turkeys are indigenous to America. In explanation of the origin of these "stealing" Rhymes I would say that it was never the Negro slave's viewpoint that his hard-earned productions righteously belonged to another. His whole viewpoint in all such cases, where he sang in this kind of verse, is well summed up in the last two lines of this little Rhyme itself:

"I tuck mysef to my tucky roos',
An' I brung *my* tucky home."

To the Negro it was his turkey. This was the Negro slave view and accounts for the origin and evolution of such verse. We leave to others a fair discussion of the ethics and a righteous conclusion; only asking them in fairness to conduct the discussion in the light of slave conditions and slave surroundings.

In a few of the Folk Rhymes one stanza will be found to be longer than any of the others. Now as to the origin of this, in the case of those sung whose tunes I happen to know, the long stanza was used as a kind of chorus, while the other stanzas were used as song "verses." I therefore think this is probably true in all cases. The reader will note that the long stanza is written first in many cases. This is because the Negro habitually begins his song with the Chorus, which is just the opposite to the custom of the Caucasian who begins his ordinary songs with the verse. This appears then to be the possible genesis of stanzas of unequal length.

I have written this little treatise on the use, origin, and evolution of the Negro Rhyme with much hesitation. I finally decided to do it only because I thought a truthful statement of fact concerning Negro Folk Rhymes might prove a help to those who are expert investigators in the field of literature and who are in search of the origin of all Folk literature and finally of all literature. The Negro being the last to come to the bright light of civilization has given or probably will give the last crop of Folk Rhymes. Human processes being largely the same, I hope that my little personal knowledge of the Negro Rhymes may help others in the other larger literary fields.

I am hoping that it may help and I am penning the last strokes to record my sincere desire that it may in no way hinder.

GENERAL INDEX

PART I

GENERAL INDEX

GENERAL INDEX

GENERAL INDEX

GENERAL INDEX

GENERAL INDEX

GENERAL INDEX

GENERAL INDEX

GENERAL INDEX

GENERAL INDEX

FOREIGN SECTION INDEX

GENERAL INDEX

PART II

COMPARATIVE STUDY INDEX

Love Songs

Dance Songs

COMPARATIVE STUDY INDEX

Animal and Nature Lore

COMPARATIVE STUDY INDEX

Nursery Rhymes

COMPARATIVE STUDY INDEX

COMPARATIVE STUDY INDEX

Charms and Superstitions

Hunting Songs

Drinking Songs

Wise and Gnomic Sayings

COMPARATIVE STUDY INDEX

Harvest Songs

Biblical and Religious Themes

Play Songs

COMPARATIVE STUDY INDEX

Miscellaneous

COMPARATIVE STUDY INDEX

COMPARATIVE STUDY INDEX

www.ingramcontent.com/pod-product-compliance
Lightning Source LLC
Chambersburg PA
CBHW040254290326
41929CB00051B/3360

* 9 7 8 1 6 3 9 2 3 7 5 2 4 *